SAMS
Teach Yourself

SQL

Ben Forta

in 10 Minutes

SAMS

A Division of Macmillan Computer Publishing
201 West 103rd St., Indianapolis, Indiana, 46290 USA

Sams Teach Yourself SQL in 10 Minutes

Copyright © 2000 by Sams Publishing

International Standard Book Number: 0-672-31664-1

Library of Congress Catalog Card Number: 99-61495

Printed in the United States of America

First Printing: September 1999

01 00   8 7 6 5

Trademarks

Warning and Disclaimer

ASSOCIATE PUBLISHER
Bradley L. Jones

ACQUISITIONS EDITOR
Sharon Cox

DEVELOPMENT EDITOR
Tom Cirtin

MANAGING EDITOR
Lisa Wilson

PROJECT EDITOR
Dawn Pearson

COPY EDITOR
Mary Lagu

INDEXER
Aamir Burki

PROOFREADER
Megan Wade

TECHNICAL EDITOR
Deanna Townsend

TEAM COORDINATOR
Meggo Barthlow

INTERIOR DESIGN
Gary Adair

COVER DESIGN
Aren Howell

COPY WRITER
Eric Borgert

LAYOUT TECHNICIANS
Lisa England
Brad Lenser
Louis Porter, Jr.

Contents

C SQL Statement Syntax 188

D SQL Datatypes 192

E SQL Reserved Words 198

Index 205

About the Author

Ben Forta is Allaire Corporation's product evangelist for the ColdFusion product line. He has over 15 years of experience in the computer industry in product development, support, training, and product marketing. Ben is the author of the popular *ColdFusion Web Application Construction Kit* and *Advanced ColdFusion 4 Development* (both published by Que) and *Sams Teach Yourself HomeSite in 24 Hours* (published by Sams). He has extensive experience in database design and development, has implemented database integration for several highly successful commercial software programs, and is a frequent lecturer and columnist on Internet and database technologies. Born in London, England, and educated in London, New York, and Los Angeles, Ben now lives in Oak Park, Michigan with his wife Marcy and their five children. Ben welcomes your email at ben@forta.com, and invites you to visit his Web site at http://www.forta.com.

Acknowledgments

First of all, I'd like to thank everyone at Macmillan who helped turn this book from a concept into a finished product.

Special thanks to my technical editor, Deanna Townsend, for her incredibly thorough review and insightful feedback. I wish all tech editors paid as much attention to detail as Deanna did.

A very special thank you to Dave Hannum, Joe Hoffman, John Elder, Marius Milosav, Martin Herbener, and Scott Raley for volunteering their valuable time to help test my SQL on as many different databases and platforms as possible. Their feedback was instrumental in making this book the unique and useful tool that it is.

And finally, because it is impossible to do this individually, thanks to all of you who encouraged me to write this book. I hope I have lived up to your expectations.

Tell Us What You Think!

As the reader of this book, *you* are our most important critic and commentator. We value your opinion and want to know what we're doing right, what we could do better, what areas you'd like to see us publish in, and any other words of wisdom you're willing to pass our way.

As an associate publisher for Sams Publishing, I welcome your comments. You can fax, email, or write me directly to let me know what you did or didn't like about this book—as well as what we can do to make our books stronger.

Please note that I cannot help you with technical problems related to the topic of this book, and that due to the high volume of mail I receive, I might not be able to reply to every message.

When you write, please be sure to include this book's title and author as well as your name and phone or fax number. I will carefully review your comments and share them with the author and editors who worked on the book.

Fax: 317-581-4770

Email: adv_prog@mcp.com

Mail: Bradley L. Jones
            Associate Publisher
            Sams Publishing
            201 West 103rd Street

Introduction

SQL is the most widely used database language. Whether you are an application developer, database administrator, Web application designer, or Microsoft Office user, a good working knowledge of SQL is an important part of interacting with databases.

There are lots of SQL books out there. Some are actually very good. But they all have one thing in common: For most users they teach just too much information. Instead of teaching SQL itself, most books teach everything from database design and normalization to relational database theory and administrative concerns. Although those are all important topics, they are not of interest to most of us who just need to learn SQL.

That is where this book comes in. *Sams Teach Yourself SQL in 10 Minutes* will teach you SQL, starting with simple data retrieval and working on to more complex topics including the use of joins, subqueries, and table constraints. You'll learn what you need to know methodically, systematically, and simply—in lessons that will each take 10 minutes or less to complete.

So turn to Lesson 1, and get to work. You'll be writing world-class SQL in no time at all.

Who is the Teach Yourself SQL book for?

This book is for you if

- You are new to SQL.

- You want to quickly learn how to get the most out of SQL.

- You want to do things quickly and easily in SQL without having to call someone for help.

Conventions Used in This Book

This book uses different typefaces to differentiate between code and regular English, and also to help you identify important concepts.

Text that you type and text that should appear on your screen is presented in monospace type.

It will look like this to mimic the way text looks on your
screen.

Placeholders for variables and expressions appear in `monospace italic` font.
You should replace the placeholder with the specific value it represents.

This arrow (➥) at the beginning of a line of code means that a single
line of code is too long to fit on the printed page. Continue typing all
characters after the ➥ as though they were part of the preceding line.

 A Note presents interesting pieces of information
related to the surrounding discussion.

 A Tip offers advice or teaches an easier way to do
something.

 A Caution advises you about potential problems and
helps you steer clear of disaster.

NEW TERM

New Term icons provide clear definitions of new, essential terms. The
term appears in italic.

INPUT

The Input icon identifies code that you can type in yourself. It usually
appears next to a listing.

OUTPUT

The Output icon highlights the output produced by running a program. It
usually appears after a listing.

ANALYSIS   The Analysis icon alerts you to the author's line-by-line analysis of a program.

LESSON 1
Understanding SQL

In this lesson, you'll learn exactly what SQL is and what it will do for you.

Database Basics

The fact that you are reading a book on SQL indicates that you, somehow, need to interact with databases. SQL is a language used to interact with databases, and so before looking at SQL itself, it is important that you understand some basic concepts about databases and database technologies.

Whether you are aware of it or not, you use databases all the time. Each time you select a name from your email address book, you are using a database. If you conduct a search on an Internet search site, you are using a database. When you log into your network at work, you are validating your name and password against a database. Even when you use your ATM card at a cash machine, you are using databases for PIN number verification and balance checking.

But even though we all use databases all the time, there remains much confusion over what exactly a database is. This is especially true because different people use the same database terms to mean different things. A good place to start our study is with a list and explanation of the most important database terms.

> **Reviewing Basic Concepts**   What follows is a very brief overview of some basic database concepts. It is intended to either jolt your memory, if you already have some database experience, or to provide you with the absolute basics, if you are new to databases. Understanding databases is an important part of mastering SQL, and you might want to find a good book on database fundamentals to brush up on the subject if needed.

Databases

The term database is used in many different ways, but for our purposes (and indeed, from SQL's perspective) a database is a collection of data stored in some organized fashion. The simplest way to think of it is to imagine a database as a filing cabinet. The filing cabinet is simply a physical location to store data, regardless of what that data is or how it is organized.

> **Database**   A container (usually a file or set of files) to store organized data.

> **Misuse Causes Confusion**   People often use the term *database* to refer to the database software they are running. This is incorrect, and it is a source of much confusion. Database software is actually called the *Database Management System* (or DBMS). The database is the container created and manipulated via the DBMS.

Tables

When you store information in your filing cabinet you don't just toss it in a drawer. Rather, you create files within the filing cabinet, and then you file related data in specific files.

In the database world, that file is called a table. A table is a structured file that can store data of a specific type. A table might contain a list customers, a product catalog, or any other list of information.

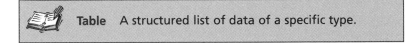

Table   A structured list of data of a specific type.

The key here is that the data stored in the table is one type of data or one list. You would never store a list of customers and a list of orders in the same database table. Rather, you'd create two tables, one for each list.

Every table in a database has a name that identifies it. That name is always unique—meaning no other table in that database can have the same name.

Columns and Datatypes

Tables are made up of columns. A column contains a particular piece of information within a table.

Column   A single field in a table. All tables are made up of one or more columns.

The best way to understand this is to envision database tables as grids, somewhat like spreadsheets. Each column in the grid contains a particular piece of information. In a customer table, for example, one column contains the customer number and another contains the customer name. The address, city, state, and zip are all stored in their own columns.

Breaking Up Data   It is extremely important to break data into multiple columns correctly. For example, city, state, and zip should always be separate columns. By breaking these out, it becomes possible to sort or filter data by specific columns (for example, to find all customers in a particular state or in a particular city). If city and state are combined into one column, it would be extremely difficult to sort or filter by state.

Each column in a database has an associated datatype. A datatype defines what type of data the column can contain. For example, if the column is to contain a number (perhaps the number of items in an order), the datatype would be a numeric datatype. If the column were to contain dates, text, notes, currency amounts, and so on, the appropriate datatype would be used to specify this.

 Datatype A type of allowed data. Every table column has an associated datatype that restricts (or allows) specific data in that column.

Rows

Data in a table is stored in rows; each record saved is stored in its own row. Again, envisioning a table as a spreadsheet style grid, the vertical columns in the grid are the table columns, and the horizontal rows are the table rows.

For example, a customers table might store one customer per row. The number of rows in the table is the number of records in it.

 Row A record in a table.

Keys

Every row in a table should have some column (or set of columns) that uniquely identifies it. A table containing customers might use a customer number column for this purpose, whereas a table containing orders might use the order ID. An employee list table might use an employee ID or the employee social security number column.

 Primary Key A column (or set of columns) whose values uniquely identify every row in a table.

This column (or set of columns) that uniquely identifies each row in a table is called a primary key. The primary key is used to refer to a single row. Without a primary key, updating or deleting specific rows in a table becomes extremely difficult.

> **Always Define Primary Keys** Although primary keys are not actually required, most database designers ensure that every table they create has a primary key so that future data manipulation is possible and manageable.

Any column in a table can be established as the primary key, as long as it meets the following conditions:

- No two rows can have the same primary key value.

- Every row must have a primary key value (column may not allow NULL values).

- The column containing primary key values can never be modified or updated.

- Primary key values can never be reused. (If a row is deleted from the table, its primary key may not be assigned to any new rows.)

Primary keys are usually defined on a single column within a table. But this is not required, and multiple columns may be used together as a primary key. When multiple columns are used the rules listed above must apply to all columns, and the values of all columns together must be unique (individual columns need not have unique values).

There is another very important type of key called a foreign key, but I'll get to that later on in Lesson 12, "Joining Tables."

What Is SQL?

SQL (pronounced as the letters S-Q-L or as *sequel*) is an abbreviation for Structured Query Language. SQL is a language designed specifically for communicating with databases.

Unlike other languages (spoken languages like English, or programming languages like C or Visual Basic), SQL is made up of very few words. This is deliberate. SQL is designed to do one thing and do it well— provide you with a simple and efficient way to read and write data from a database.

What are the advantages of SQL?

- SQL is not a proprietary language used by individual database vendors. Almost every major database supports SQL, so learning this one language will enable you to interact with almost every major database out there.

- SQL is easy to learn. The statements are all made up of descriptive English words, and there aren't that many of them.

- Despite its apparent simplicity, SQL is actually a very powerful language, and by cleverly using its language elements you can perform very complex and sophisticated database operations.

And with that, let's learn SQL.

SQL Extensions   Many DBMS vendors have extended their support for SQL by adding statements or instructions to the language. The purpose of these extensions is to provide extra functionality or simplified ways to perform specific operations. And while often extremely useful, these extensions tend to be very DBMS specific, and they are rarely supported by more than a single vendor.

Standard SQL is governed by the ANSI standards committee, and is thus called ANSI SQL. All major DBMSs, even those with their own extensions, support ANSI SQL. Individual implementations have their own names (PL-SQL, Transact-SQL, and so forth).

For the most part, the SQL taught in this book is ANSI SQL. On the odd occasion where DBMS specific SQL is used it is so noted.

Summary

In this first lesson, you learned what SQLis ans why it is useful. Because SQL is used to interact with databases, you also reviewed some basic database terminology.

LESSON 2
Retrieving Data

In this lesson, you'll learn how to use the SELECT *statement to retrieve one or more columns of data from a table.*

The SELECT Statement

As explained in Lesson 1, "Understanding SQL," SQL statements are made up of plain English terms. These terms are called keywords, and every SQL statement is made up of one or more keywords. The SQL statement that you'll probably use most frequently is the SELECT statement. Its purpose is to retrieve information from one or more tables.

 Keyword A reserved word that is part of the SQL language. Never name a table or column using a keyword. Appendix E, "SQL Reserved Words," lists some of the more common reserved words.

To use SELECT to retrieve table data you must, at minimum, specify two pieces of information—what you want to select, and from where you want to select it.

> **Following Along with the Examples** The sample SQL statements (and sample output) throughout the lessons in this book use a set of data files that are described in Appendix A, "Sample Table Scripts." If you'd like to follow along and try the examples yourself (I strongly recommend that you do so), refer to Appendix A. It contains sample scripts that you can use to create these data files, as well as for instructions about where you can go to download complete, populated, sample files.
>
> It is important to understand that SQL is a language, not an application. The way that you specify SQL statements and display statement output varies from one application to the next. To assist you in adapting the examples to your own environment, Appendix B, "Working in Popular Applications," explains how to issue the statements taught throughout this book using many popular applications and development environments.

Retrieving Individual Columns

We'll start with a simple SQL SELECT statement, as follows:

INPUT

```
SELECT prod_name
FROM Products;
```

ANALYSIS

The statement above uses the SELECT statement to retrieve a single column called prod_name from the products table. The desired column name is specified right after the SELECT keyword, and the FROM keyword specifies the name of the table from which to retrieve the data. The output from this statement is shown following:

OUTPUT

```
prod_name
--------------------
Fish bean bag toy
Bird bean bag toy
Rabbit bean bag toy
8 inch teddy bear
12 inch teddy bear
18 inch teddy bear
Raggedy Ann
```

A simple SELECT statement similar to the one used above returns all the rows in a table. Data is not filtered, nor is it sorted. We'll discuss these topics in the next few lessons.

Terminating Statements   Multiple SQL statements must be separated by semicolons (the ; character). Most DBMSs do not require that a semicolon be specified after single statements. But if your particular DBMS complains, you might have to add it there. Of course, you can always add a semicolon if you wish. It'll do no harm, even if it is, in fact, not needed.

SQL Statement and Case   It is important to note that SQL statements are case-insensitive, so SELECT is the same as select, which is the same as Select. Many SQL developers find that using uppercase for all SQL keywords and lowercase for column and table names makes code easier to read and debug.

Use of Whitespace   All extra whitespace within a SQL statement is ignored when that statement is processed. SQL statements can be specified on one long line or broken up over many lines. Most SQL developers find that breaking up statements over multiple lines makes them easier to read and debug.

Retrieving Multiple Columns

To retrieve multiple columns from a table, the same SELECT statement is used. The only difference is that multiple column names must be specified after the SELECT keyword, and each column must be separated by a comma.

 Take Care with Commas When selecting multiple columns be sure to specify a comma between each column name, but not after the last column name. Doing so will generate an error.

The following SELECT statement retrieves three columns from the products table:

INPUT

```
SELECT prod_id, prod_name, prod_price
FROM Products;
```

ANALYSIS

Just as in the prior example, this statement uses the SELECT statement to retrieve data from the products table. In this example, three column names are specified, each separated by a comma. The output from this statement is shown below:

OUTPUT

```
prod_id     prod_name              prod_price
---------   --------------------   ----------
BNBG01      Fish bean bag toy        3.4900
BNBG02      Bird bean bag toy        3.4900
BNBG03      Rabbit bean bag toy      3.4900
BR01        8 inch teddy bear        5.9900
BR02        12 inch teddy bear       8.9900
BR03        18 inch teddy bear      11.9900
RGAN01      Raggedy Ann              4.9900
```

> *Presentation of Data* As you will notice in the above output, SQL statements typically return raw, unformatted data. Data formatting is a presentation issue, not a retrieval issue. Therefore, presentations (for example, displaying the above price values as currency amounts with the correct number of decimal places) are specified in the application that displays the data. Actual retrieved data (without application-provided formatting) is rarely used.

Retrieving All Columns

In addition to being able to specify desired columns (one or more, as seen above), SELECT statements can also request all columns without having to list them individually. This is done using the asterisk (*) wildcard character in lieu of actual column names, as follows:

`INPUT`

```
SELECT *
FROM Products;
```

When a wildcard (*) is specified, all the columns in the table are returned. The column order will typically, but not always, be the physical order in which the columns appear in the table definition. However, SQL data is seldom displayed as is. (Usually, it is returned to an application that formats or presents the data as needed.) This does should not pose a problem.

> *Using Wildcards* As a rule, you are better off not using the * wildcard unless you really do need every column in the table. Even though use of wildcards may save you the time and effort needed to list the desired columns explicitly, retrieving unnecessary columns usually slows down the performance of your retrieval and your application.

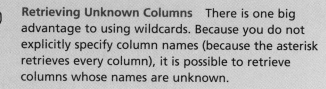

> **Retrieving Unknown Columns**   There is one big
> advantage to using wildcards. Because you do not
> explicitly specify column names (because the asterisk
> retrieves every column), it is possible to retrieve
> columns whose names are unknown.

Summary

In this lesson, you learned how to use the SQL SELECT statement to
retrieve a single table column, multiple table columns, and all table
columns. Next you'll learn how to sort the retrieved data.

LESSON 3

Sorting Retrieved Data

In this lesson, you will learn how to use the SELECT *statement's* ORDER BY *clause to sort retrieved data as needed.*

Sorting Data

As you learned in the last lesson, the following SQL statement returns a single column from a database table. But look at the output. The data appears to be displayed in no particular order at all.

INPUT

```
SELECT prod_name
FROM Products;
```

OUTPUT

```
prod_name
--------------------
Fish bean bag toy
Bird bean bag toy
Rabbit bean bag toy
8 inch teddy bear
12 inch teddy bear
18 inch teddy bear
Raggedy Ann
```

Actually, the retrieved data is not displayed in a mere random order. If left unsorted, data will be displayed in the order in which it appears in the underlying tables. This could be the order in which the data was added to the tables initially. However, if data was subsequently updated or deleted, the order will be affected by how the DBMS reuses reclaimed storage space. The end result is that you cannot (and should not) rely on the sort order if you do not explicitly control it. Relational database design theory states that the sequence of retrieved data cannot be assumed to have significance if ordering was not explicitly specified.

To explicitly sort data retrieved using a SELECT statement, the ORDER BY clause is used. ORDER BY takes the name of one or more columns by which to sort the output. Look at the following example:

INPUT

```
SELECT prod_name
FROM Products
ORDER BY prod_name;
```

ANALYSIS This statement is identical to the earlier statement, except it also specifies an ORDER BY clause instructing the Database Management System software to sort the data by the prod_name column. The results are as follows:

OUTPUT

```
prod_name
--------------------
12 inch teddy bear
18 inch teddy bear
8 inch teddy bear
Bird bean bag toy
Fish bean bag toy
Rabbit bean bag toy
Raggedy Ann
```

Position of ORDER BY Clause When specifying an ORDER BY clause, be sure that it is the last clause in your SELECT statement. If it is not the last clause, an error will be generated.

Sorting by Multiple Columns

It is often necessary to sort data by more than one column. For example, if you are displaying an employee list, you might want to display it sorted by last name and first name (first by last name, and then within each last name sort by first name). This would be useful if there are multiple employees with the same last name.

To sort by multiple columns, simply specify the column names separated by commas (just as you do when you are selecting multiple columns).

The following code retrieves three columns and sorts the results by two of them—first by price and then by name.

INPUT

```
SELECT prod_id, prod_price, prod_name
FROM Products
ORDER BY prod_price, prod_name;
```

OUTPUT

```
prod_id       prod_price      prod_name
-------       ----------      --------------------
BNBG02        3.4900          Bird bean bag toy
BNBG01        3.4900          Fish bean bag toy
BNBG03        3.4900          Rabbit bean bag toy
RGAN01        4.9900          Raggedy Ann
BR01          5.9900          8 inch teddy bear
BR02          8.9900          12 inch teddy bear
BR03          11.9900         18 inch teddy bear
```

It is important to understand that when you are sorting by multiple columns, the sort sequence is exactly as specified. In other words, using the output in the example above, the products are sorted by the prod_name column only (if the prod_price value is the same). If all the values in the

prod_price column had been unique, no data would have been sorted by
prod_name.

Sorting by Column Position

In addition to being able to specify sort order using column names, ORDER
BY also supports ordering specified by relative column position. The best
way to understand this is to look at an example:

INPUT

```
SELECT prod_id, prod_price, prod_name
FROM Products
ORDER BY 2, 3;
```

OUTPUT

```
prod_id      prod_price     prod_name
-------      ----------     -------------------
BNBG02       3.4900         Bird bean bag toy
BNBG01       3.4900         Fish bean bag toy
BNBG03       3.4900         Rabbit bean bag toy
RGAN01       4.9900         Raggedy Ann
BR01         5.9900         8 inch teddy bear
BR02         8.9900         12 inch teddy bear
BR03         11.9900        18 inch teddy bear
```

ANALYSIS   As you can see, the output is identical to that of the query
above. The difference here is in the ORDER BY clause. Instead of specifying
column names, the relative positions of selected columns in the SELECT list
are specified. ORDER BY 2 means sort by the second column in the SELECT
list. ORDER BY 2, 3 means sort by prod_price and then by prod_name.

The primary advantage of this technique is that it saves retyping the column names. The downside is that it is all too easy to mistakenly reorder
data when making changes to the SELECT list.

> **Sorting by Nonselected Columns**   Obviously, this
> technique cannot be used when sorting by columns
> that do not appear in the SELECT list. However, you
> can mix and match actual column names and relative
> column positions in a single statement if needed.

Specifying Sort Direction

Data sorting is not limited to ascending sort orders (from A to Z). Although this is the default sort order, the ORDER BY clause can also be used to sort in descending order (from Z to A). To sort by descending order, the keyword DESC must be specified.

The following example sorts the products in descending order (most expensive first), plus product name:

INPUT

```
SELECT prod_id, prod_price, prod_name
FROM Products
ORDER BY prod_price DESC, prod_name;
```

OUTPUT

```
prod_id      prod_price   prod_name
-------      ----------   -------------------
BR03         11.9900      18 inch teddy bear
BR02         8.9900       12 inch teddy bear
BR01         5.9900       8 inch teddy bear
RGAN01       4.9900       Raggedy Ann
BNBG02       3.4900       Bird bean bag toy
BNBG01       3.4900       Fish bean bag toy
BNBG03       3.4900       Rabbit bean bag toy
```

The DESC keyword only applies to the column name that directly precedes it. In the example above, DESC was specified for the prod_price column, but not for the prod_name column. Therefore, the prod_price column is sorted in descending order, but the prod_name column (within each price) is still sorted in standard ascending order.

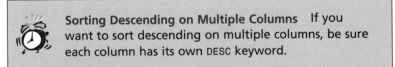

Sorting Descending on Multiple Columns   If you want to sort descending on multiple columns, be sure each column has its own DESC keyword.

It is worth noting that DESC is short for DESCENDING, and both keywords may be used. The opposite of DESC is ASC (or ASCENDING), which may be specified to sort in ascending order. In practice, however, ASC is not usually used because ascending order is the default sequence (and is assumed if neither ASC nor DESC are specified).

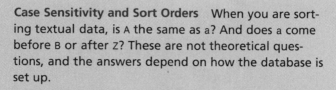

Case Sensitivity and Sort Orders When you are sorting textual data, is A the same as a? And does a come before B or after Z? These are not theoretical questions, and the answers depend on how the database is set up.

In *dictionary* sort order, A is treated the same as a, and that is the default behavior for most Database Management Systems. However, most good DBMSs enable database administrators to change this behavior if needed. (If your database contains lots of foreign language characters, this might become necessary.)

The key here is that, if you do need an alternate sort order, you cannot accomplish it with a simple ORDER BY clause. You must contact your database administrator.

Summary

In this lesson, you learned how to sort retrieved data using the SELECT statement's ORDER BY clause. This clause, which must be the last in the SELECT statement, can be used to sort data on one or more columns as needed.

LESSON 4
Filtering Data

In this lesson, you will learn how to use the SELECT *statement's* WHERE
clause to specify search conditions.

Using the WHERE Clause

Database tables usually contain large amounts of data, and you seldom
need to retrieve all the rows in a table. More often than not you'll want to
extract a subset of the table's data as needed for specific operations or
reports. Retrieving just the data you want involves specifying *search
criteria*, also known as a *filter condition*.

Within a SELECT statement, data is filtered by specifying search criteria in
the WHERE clause. The WHERE clause is specified right after the table name
(the FROM clause) as follows:

INPUT

```
SELECT prod_name, prod_price
FROM Products
WHERE prod_price = 3.49;
```

ANALYSIS

This statement retrieves two columns from the products table, but instead
of returning all rows, only rows with a prod_price value of 3.49 are
returned, as follows:

OUTPUT

```
prod_name                    prod_price
-------------------          ----------
Fish bean bag toy            3.4900
Bird bean bag toy            3.4900
Rabbit bean bag toy          3.4900
```

This example uses a simple equality test: it checks to see if a column has a specified value, and it filters the data accordingly. But SQL lets you do more than just test for equality.

SQL versus Application Filtering   Data can also be filtered at the application level. To do this, the SQL SELECT statement retrieves more data than is actually required for the client application, and the client code loops through the returned data to extract just the needed rows.

As a rule, this practice is strongly discouraged. Databases are optimized to perform filtering quickly and efficiently. Making the client application (or development language) do the databases job will dramatically impact application performance and will create applications that cannot scale properly. In addition, if data is filtered at the client, the server has to send unneeded data across the network connections, resulting in a waste of network bandwidth usage.

WHERE Clause Position   When using both ORDER BY and WHERE clauses, make sure that ORDER BY comes after the WHERE, otherwise an error will be generated. (See Lesson 3, "Sorting Retrieved Data," for more information on using ORDER BY.)

The WHERE Clause Operators

The first WHERE clause we looked at tests for equality—determining if a column contains a specific value. SQL supports a whole range of conditional operators as listed in Table 4.1.

TABLE 4.1 WHERE Clause Operators

Operator	Description
=	Equality
<>	Non-equality
!=	Non-equality
<	Less than
<=	Less than or equal to
!<	Not less than
>	Greater than
>=	Greater than or equal to
!>	Not greater than
BETWEEN	Between two specified values
IS NULL	Is a NULL value

Operator Compatibility   Some of the operators listed in Table 4.1 are redundant (for example, <> is the same as !=. !< (not less than) accomplishes the same effect as >= (greater than or equal to). Not all of these operators are supported by all DBMSs. Refer to your DBMS documentation to determine exactly what it supports.

Checking Against a Single Value

We have already seen an example of testing for equality. Let's take a look at a few examples to demonstrate the use of other operators.

This first example lists all products that cost less than $10:

INPUT

```
SELECT prod_name, prod_price
FROM Products
WHERE prod_price < 10;
```

OUTPUT

```
prod_name                  prod_price
------------------         ----------
Fish bean bag toy          3.4900
Bird bean bag toy          3.4900
Rabbit bean bag toy        3.4900
8 inch teddy bear          5.9900
12 inch teddy bear         8.9900
Raggedy Ann                4.9900
```

Checking For Nonmatches

This next example lists all products not made by vendor DLL01:

INPUT

```
SELECT vend_id, prod_name
FROM Products
WHERE vend_id <> 'DLL01';
```

OUTPUT

```
vend_id     prod_name
----------  -------------------
BRS01       8 inch teddy bear
BRS01       12 inch teddy bear
BRS01       18 inch teddy bear
```

> **When to Use Quotes**   If you look closely at the condi-
> tions used in the above WHERE clauses, you will notice
> that some values are enclosed within single quotes,
> and others are not. The single quotes are used to
> delimit a string. If you are comparing a value against
> a column that is a string datatype, the delimiting
> quotes are required. Quotes are not used to delimit
> values used with numeric columns.

Checking for a Range of Values

To check for a range of values, you can use the BETWEEN operator. Its syntax is a little different from other WHERE clause operators because it
requires two values: the beginning and end of the range. The BETWEEN

operator can be used, for example, to check for all products that cost between $5 and $10 or for all dates that fall between specified start and end dates.

The following example demonstrates the use of the BETWEEN operator by retrieving all products with a price between $5 and $10:

INPUT

```
SELECT prod_name, prod_price
FROM Products
WHERE prod_price BETWEEN 5 AND 10;
```

OUTPUT

```
prod_name              prod_price
-----------------      ----------
8 inch teddy bear      5.9900
12 inch teddy bear     8.9900
```

ANALYSIS   As seen in this example, when BETWEEN is used, two values must be specified—the low end and high end of the desired range. The two values must also be separated by the AND keyword. BETWEEN matches all the values in the range, including the specified start and end values.

Checking for No Value

When a table is created, the table designer can specify whether or not individual columns can contain no value. When a column contains no value, it is said to contain a NULL value.

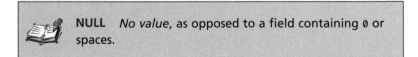

NULL   *No value*, as opposed to a field containing 0 or spaces.

The SELECT statement has a special WHERE clause that can be used to check for columns with NULL values—the IS NULL clause. The syntax looks like this:

INPUT

```
SELECT prod_name
FROM Products
WHERE prod_price IS NULL;
```

ANALYSIS This statement returns a list of all products that have no price (an empty prod_price field, not a price of 0), and because there are none, no data is returned.

> **DBMS Specific Operators** Many DBMSs extend the standard set of operators, providing advanced filtering options. Refer to your DBMS documentation for more information.

Summary

In this lesson, you learned how to filter returned data using the SELECT statement's WHERE clause. You learned how to test for equality, nonequality, greater than and less than value ranges, as well as for NULL values.

LESSON 5

Advanced Data Filtering

In this lesson, you'll learn how to combine WHERE clauses to create power-ful and sophisticated search conditions. You'll also learn how to use the NOT and IN operators.

Combining WHERE Clauses

All the WHERE clauses introduced in Lesson 4, "Filtering Data," filter data using a single criteria. For a greater degree of filter control, SQL lets you specify multiple WHERE clauses. These clauses may be used in two ways: as AND clauses or as OR clauses.

Using the AND Operator

To filter by more than one column, you use the AND operator to append conditions to your WHERE clause. The following code demonstrates this:

INPUT

```
SELECT prod_name, prod_price
FROM Products
WHERE vend_id = 'DLL01' AND prod_price <= 4;
```

ANALYSIS The above SQL statement retrieves the product name and price for all products made by vendor DLL01 as long as the price is $4 or less. The WHERE clause in this SELECT statement is made up of two conditions, and the keyword AND is used to join them. AND instructs the database man-agement system software to return only rows that meet all the conditions specified. If a product is made be vendor DLL01, but it costs more than $4, it is not retrieved. Similarly, products that cost less than $4 that are made by a vendor other than the one specified are not to be retrieved. The out-put generated by this SQL statement is as follows:

```
prod_name            prod_price
------------------   ----------
Fish bean bag toy    3.4900
Bird bean bag toy    3.4900
Rabbit bean bag toy  3.4900
```

 AND A keyword used in a WHERE clause to specify that only rows matching all the specified conditions should be retrieved.

Using the OR Operator

The OR operator is exactly the opposite of AND. The OR operator instructs the database management system software to retrieve rows that match either condition. In fact, most better DBMSs will not even evaluate the second condition in an OR WHERE clause if the first condition has already been met. (If the first condition was met, the row would be retrieved regardless of the second condition.)

Look at the following SELECT statement:

```
SELECT prod_name, prod_price
FROM Products
WHERE vend_id = 'DLL01' OR vend_id = 'BRS01';
```

ANALYSIS The above SQL statement retrieves the product name and price for any products made by either of the two specified vendors. The OR operator tells the DBMS to match either condition, not both. If an AND operator is used here, no data is returned. The output generated by this SQL statement is as follows:

```
prod_name            prod_price
------------------   ----------
Fish bean bag toy    3.4900
Bird bean bag toy    3.4900
Rabbit bean bag toy  3.4900
8 inch teddy bear    5.9900
```

```
12 inch teddy bear     8.9900
18 inch teddy bear     11.9900
Raggedy Ann            4.9900
```

 OR   A keyword used in a WHERE clause to specify that any rows matching either of the specified conditions should be retrieved.

Understanding Order of Evaluation

WHERE clauses can contain any number of AND and OR operators. Combining the two enables you to perform sophisticated and complex filtering.

But combining AND and OR operators presents an interesting problem. To demonstrate this, look at an example. You need a list of all products costing $10 or more made by vendors DLL01 and BRS01. The following SELECT statement uses a combination of AND and OR operators to build a WHERE clause:

INPUT

```
SELECT prod_name, prod_price
FROM Products
WHERE vend_id = 'DLL01' OR vend_id = 'BRS01' AND prod_price >=
➥10;
```

OUTPUT

```
prod_name               prod_price
------------------      ----------
Fish bean bag toy       3.4900
Bird bean bag toy       3.4900
Rabbit bean bag toy     3.4900
18 inch teddy bear      11.9900
Raggedy Ann             4.9900
```

ANALYSIS   Look at the results above. Four of the rows returned have prices less than $10—so, obviously, the rows were not filtered as intended. Why did this happen? The answer is the order of evaluation. SQL (like most languages) processes AND operators before OR operators. When SQL sees the above WHERE clause, it reads *any products costing $10 or more made by vendor* BRS01, *and any products made by vendor* DLL01 *regardless of price*. In other words, because AND ranks higher in the order of evaluation, the wrong operators were joined together.

The solution to this problem is to use parenthesis to explicitly group related operators. Take a look at the following SELECT statement and output:

INPUT

```
SELECT prod_name, prod_price
FROM Products
WHERE (vend_id = 'DLL01' OR vend_id = 'BRS01') AND prod_price
➥>= 10;
```

OUTPUT

```
prod_name              prod_price
------------------     ----------
18 inch teddy bear     11.9900
```

ANALYSIS The only difference between this SELECT statement and the earlier one is that, in this statement, the first two WHERE clause conditions are enclosed within parenthesis. As parenthesis have a higher order of evaluation than either AND or OR operators, the DBMS first filters the OR condition within those parenthesis. The SQL statement then becomes *any products made by either vendor* DLL01 *or vendor* BRS01 *costing $10 or greater*, which is exactly what we want.

> **Using Parenthesis in WHERE Clauses** Whenever you write WHERE clauses that use both AND and OR operators, use parenthesis to explicitly group operators. Don't ever rely on the default evaluation order, even if it is exactly what you want. There is no downside to using parenthesis, and you are always better off eliminating any ambiguity.

Using the IN Operator

The IN operator is used to specify a range of conditions, any of which can be matched. IN takes a comma-delimited list of valid values, all enclosed within parenthesis. The following input demonstrates this:

INPUT

```
SELECT prod_name, prod_price
FROM Products
WHERE vend_id  IN ('DLL01','BRS01')
ORDER BY prod_name;
```

OUTPUT

```
prod_name               prod_price
------------------      ----------
12 inch teddy bear      8.99
18 inch teddy bear      11.99
8 inch teddy bear       5.99
Bird bean bag toy       3.49
Fish bean bag toy       3.49
Rabbit bean bag toy     3.49
Raggedy Ann             4.99
```

ANALYSIS   The SELECT statement retrieves all products made by vendor DLL01 and vendor BRS01. The IN operator is followed by a comma-delimited list of valid values, and the entire list must be enclosed within parenthesis.

If you are thinking that the IN operator accomplishes the same goal as OR, you are right. The following SQL statement accomplishes the exact same thing as the example above:

INPUT

```
SELECT prod_name, prod_price
FROM Products
WHERE vend_id  = 'DLL01' OR vend_id = 'BRS01'
ORDER BY prod_name;
```

OUTPUT

```
prod_name               prod_price
------------------      ----------
12 inch teddy bear      8.99
18 inch teddy bear      11.99
```

```
8 inch teddy bear        5.99
Bird bean bag toy        3.49
Fish bean bag toy        3.49
Rabbit bean bag toy      3.49
Raggedy Ann              4.99
```

Why use the IN operator? The advantages are

- When you are working with long lists of valid options, the IN operator syntax is far cleaner and easier to read.

- The order of evaluation is easier to manage when IN is used in conjunction with other AND and OR operators.

- IN operators almost always execute more quickly than lists of OR operators.

- The biggest advantage of IN is that the IN operator can contain another SELECT statement, enabling you to build highly dynamic WHERE clauses. You'll look at this in detail in Lesson 11, "Working with Subqueries."

Using the NOT Operator

The WHERE clause's NOT operator has one function and one function only—NOT negates whatever condition comes next. Because NOT is never used by itself (it is always used in conjunction with some other operator), its syntax is a little different from all other operators. Unlike other operators, the NOT keyword can be used before the column to filter on, not just after it.

The following example demonstrates the use of NOT. To list the products made by all vendors except vendor DLL01, you can write the following:

INPUT

```
SELECT prod_name
FROM Products
WHERE NOT vend_id   = 'DLL01'
ORDER BY prod_name;
```

OUTPUT

```
prod_name
-----------------
12 inch teddy bear
18 inch teddy bear
8 inch teddy bear
```

ANALYSIS The NOT here negates the condition that follows it; so instead of matching vend_id to DLL01, the DBMS matches vend_id to anything that is not DLL01.

The preceding example could have also been accomplished using the <> operator, as follows:

INPUT

```
SELECT prod_name
FROM Products
WHERE vend_id  <> 'DLL01'
ORDER BY prod_name;
```

OUTPUT

```
prod_name
-----------------
12 inch teddy bear
18 inch teddy bear
8 inch teddy bear
```

ANALYSIS Why use NOT? Well, for simple WHERE clauses such as the ones shown here, there really is no advantage to using NOT. NOT is useful in more complex clauses. For example, using NOT in conjunction with an IN operator makes it simple to find all rows that do not match a list of criteria.

Summary

This lesson picked up where the last lesson left off and taught you how to combine WHERE clauses with the AND and OR operators. You also learned how to explicitly manage the order of evaluation and how to use the IN and NOT operators.

LESSON 6
Using Wildcard Filtering

In this lesson, you'll learn what wildcards are, how they are used, and how to perform wildcard searches using the LIKE *operator for sophisticated filtering of retrieved data.*

Using the **LIKE** Operator

All the previous operators we studied filter against known values. Be it matching one or more values, testing for greater-than or less-than known values, or checking a range of values, the common denominator is that the values used in the filtering are known.

But filtering data that way does not always work. For example, how could you search for all products that contained the text *bean bag* within the product name? That cannot be done with simple comparison operators; that's a job for wildcard searching. Using wildcards, you can create search patterns that can be compared against your data. In this example, if you want to find all products that contain the words *bean bag*, you can construct a wildcard search pattern enabling you to find that *bean bag* text anywhere within a product name.

 Wildcards Special characters use to match parts of a value.

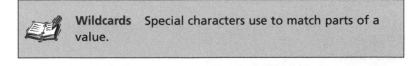 **Search pattern** A search condition made up of literal text and one or more wildcard characters.

The wildcards themselves are actually characters that have special meanings within SQL WHERE clauses, and SQL supports several different wildcard types.

To use wildcards in search clauses, the LIKE operator must be used. LIKE instructs the DBMS that the following search pattern is to be compared using a wildcard match rather than a straight equality match.

The Percent Sign (%) Wildcard

The most frequently used wildcard is the percent sign (%). Within a search string, % means, *match any number of occurrences of any character*. For example, to find all products that started with the word *fish*, you can issue the following SELECT statement:

`INPUT`

```
SELECT prod_id, prod_name
FROM Products
WHERE prod_name LIKE 'fish%';
```

`OUTPUT`

```
prod_id    prod_name
-------    ----------------
BNBG01     Fish bean bag toy
```

`ANALYSIS` This example uses a search pattern of 'fish%'. When this clause is evaluated, any value that starts with fish will be retrieved. The % tells the DBMS to accept any characters after the word fish, regardless of how many characters there are.

Wildcards can be used anywhere within the search pattern, and multiple wildcards may be used as well. The following example uses two wildcards, one at either end of the pattern:

`INPUT`

```
SELECT prod_id, prod_name
FROM Products
WHERE prod_name LIKE '%bean bag%';
```

OUTPUT

```
prod_id     prod_name
--------    --------------------
BNBG01      Fish bean bag toy
BNBG02      Bird bean bag toy
BNBG03      Rabbit bean bag toy
```

ANALYSIS The search pattern '%bean bag%' means *match any value that contains the text* bean bag *anywhere within it, regardless of any characters before or after that text.*

It is important to note that, in addition to matching one or more characters, % also matches *zero* characters. % represents zero, one, or more characters at the specified location in the search pattern.

The Underscore (_) Wildcard

Another useful wildcard is the underscore (_). The underscore is used just like %, but instead of matching multiple characters the underscore matches just a single character.

Take a look at this example:

INPUT

```
SELECT prod_id, prod_name
FROM Products
WHERE prod_name LIKE '__ inch teddy bear';
```

OUTPUT

```
prod_id     prod_name
--------    --------------------
BNBG02      12 inch teddy bear
BNBG03      18 inch teddy bear
```

ANALYSIS The search pattern used in this WHERE clause specified two wildcards followed by literal text. The results shown are the only rows that match the search pattern: The underscore matches 12 in the first row and 18 in the second row. The 8 inch teddy bear product did not match because the search pattern required two wildcard matches, not one. By contrast, the following SELECT statement uses the % wildcard and returns three matching products:

INPUT

```
SELECT prod_id, prod_name
FROM Products
WHERE prod_name LIKE '% inch teddy bear';
```

OUTPUT

```
prod_id    prod_name
--------   --------------------
BNBG01     8 inch teddy bear
BNBG02     12 inch teddy bear
BNBG03     18 inch teddy bear
```

The Brackets ([]) Wildcard

The brackets ([]) wildcard is used to specify a set of characters, any one of which must match a character in the specified position (the location of the wildcard). For example, to find all contacts whose names begin with the letter J or the letter M, you can do the following:

INPUT

```
SELECT cust_contact
FROM Customers
WHERE cust_contact LIKE '[JM]%'
ORDER BY cust_contact;
```

OUTPUT

```
cust_contact
----------------
Jim Jones
John Smith
Michelle Green
```

ANALYSIS   The WHERE clause in this statement is '[JM]%'. This search pattern uses two different wildcards. The [JM] matches any contact name that begins with either of the letters within the brackets, and it also matches only a single character. Therefore, any names longer than one character will not match. The % wildcard after the [JM] matches any number of characters after the first character, returning the desired results.

Caution The brackets ([ ]) wildcard is not supported by all DBMSs. Consult your DBMS documentation to find out if this particular wildcard is supported.

Tips for Using Wildcards

As you can see, SQL's wildcards are extremely powerful. But that power comes with a price: wildcard searches typically take far longer to process than any other search types discussed previously. Here are some rules to keep in mind when using wildcards:

- Don't overuse wildcards. If another search operator will do, use it instead.

- When you do use wildcards, try to not use them at the beginning of the search pattern unless absolutely necessary. Search patterns that begin with wildcards are the slowest to process.

- Pay careful attention to the placement of the wildcard symbols. If they are misplaced, you might not return the data you intended.

Having said that, wildcards are an important and useful search tool, and one that you will use frequently.

Summary

In this lesson, you learned what wildcards are and how to use SQL wildcards within your WHERE clauses. You also learned that wildcards should be used carefully and never overused.

LESSON 7

Creating Calculated Fields

In this lesson, you will learn what calculated fields are, how to create them, and how to use aliases to refer to them from within your application.

Understanding Calculated Fields

Data stored within a databases tables is often not available in the exact format needed by your applications. Here are some examples:

- City, State, and Zip are stored in separate columns (as they should be), but your mailing label printing program needs them retrieved as one correctly formatted field.

- Column data is in mixed upper- and lowercase, and your report needs all data presented in uppercase.

- An Order Items table stores item price and quantity, but not the expanded price (price multiplied by quantity) of each item. To print invoices, you need that expanded price.

- You need total, averages, or other calculations based on table data.

In each of these examples, the data stored in the table is not exactly what your application needs. Rather than retrieve the data as it is, and then reformat it within your client application or report, what you really want is to retrieve converted, calculated, or reformatted data directly from the database.

This is where calculated fields come in. Unlike all the columns that we retrieved in the lessons thus far, calculated fields don't actually exist in database tables. Rather, a calculated field is created on-the-fly within a SQL SELECT statement.

> **Field** Essentially means the same thing as *column* and often used interchangeably, although database columns are typically called *columns* and the term *fields* is usually used in conjunction with calculated fields.

It is important to note that only the database knows which columns in a SELECT statement are actual table columns and which are calculated fields. From the perspective of a client (for example, your application), a calculated field's data is returned in the same way as data from any other column.

> **Client Versus Server Formatting** Many of the conversions and reformatting that can be performed within SQL statements can also be performed directly in your client application. However, as a rule, it is far quicker to perform these operations on the database server than it is to perform them within the client.

Concatenating Fields

To demonstrate working with calculated fields, let's start with a simple example—the mailing address.

The Vendors table contains vendor name and address information. Imagine that you are sending out a mailing to all your vendors and that you are printing labels using a report you have created. The label report requires three lines of text—the vendor name and two address lines.

The SELECT statement that returns all the vendor names is simple enough, but how would you create the second address line? The label application wants a single value, and the data in the table is stored in three columns: vend_city, vend_state, and vend_zip.

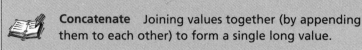

Concatenate   Joining values together (by appending them to each other) to form a single long value.

The solution is to concatenate the three columns. In SQL SELECT statements, you can concatenate columns using a special operator. Depending on what DBMS you are using, this can be a plus sign (+) or two pipes (¦¦). Here's an example (using the plus sign, the syntax used by Microsoft SQL Server, Microsoft Access, and Sybase):

INPUT

```
SELECT vend_city+', '+vend_state+' '+vend_zip
FROM Vendors
ORDER BY vend_name;
```

OUTPUT

```
- - - - - - - - - - - - - - - - - - - - - - - - - - - - - - - - - - - - - - - - - - - - - - - - -
Anytown            ,          OH        44333
Bear Town          ,          MI        44444
Dollsville         ,          CA        99999
New York           ,          NY        11111
```

INPUT

The following is the Oracle version of the same statement:

```
SELECT vend_city ¦¦ ', ' ¦¦ vend_state ¦¦ ' ' ¦¦ vend_zip
FROM Vendors
ORDER BY vend_name;
```

OUTPUT

```
- - - - - - - - - - - - - - - - - - - - - - - - - - - - - - - - - - - - - - - - - - - - - - - - -
Anytown               ,          OH        44333
```

```
Bear Town        ,        MI        44444
Dollsville       ,        CA        99999
New York         ,        NY        11111
```

ANALYSIS The above SELECT statements concatenate the following elements:

- The city stored in the vend_city column.

- A string containing a comma and a space that will go between the City and State columns.

- The state stored in the vend_state column.

- A string containing a space that will go between the State and Zip columns.

- The Zip code stored in the vend_zip column.

As you can see in the output shown above, the SELECT statement returns a single column (a calculated field) containing all these five elements as one unit.

> **Note for Oracle Users** If you are using Oracle, you will need to use two pipes (¦¦) as the concatenation operator. Oracle does this to distinguish between addition and concatenation.
>
> So how do DBMSs that use a plus sign (+) for concatenation know when to interpret the sign as addition and when to treat it as concatenation? It depends on the column datatypes. If the datatypes are numeric, SQL will add them together (a mathematical addition). If they are textual datatypes (which cannot be mathematically added), SQL concatenates the values instead. For a discussion on datatypes, see Lesson 1, "Understanding SQL."

Look again at the output returned by the SELECT statement. The three
columns that are incorporated into the calculated field are padded with
spaces. Many databases (although not all) save text values padded to the
column width. To return the data formatted properly, you must trim those
padded spaces. This can be done using the SQL RTRIM() function, as
follows:

INPUT

```
SELECT RTRIM(vend_city)+', '+RTRIM(vend_state)+'
➡'+RTRIM(vend_zip)
FROM Vendors
ORDER BY vend_name;
```

OUTPUT

```
------------------------------------------------------------------
Anytown, OH 44333
Bear Town, MI 44444
Dollsville, CA 99999
New York, NY 11111
```

Here's the Oracle version:

INPUT

```
SELECT RTRIM(vend_city) ¦¦ ', ' ¦¦ RTRIM(vend_state) ¦¦ ' ' ¦¦
➡RTRIM(vend_zip)
FROM Vendors
ORDER BY vend_name;
```

OUTPUT

```
------------------------------------------------------------------
Anytown, OH 44333
Bear Town, MI 44444
Dollsville, CA 99999
New York, NY 11111
```

The RTRIM() function trims all space from the right of a value. By using
ANALYSIS RTRIM(), the individual columns are all trimmed properly. A
comma and space separate the city and state, and a space separates the
State and Zip.

Using Aliases

The SELECT statement used to concatenate the address field works well, as seen in the above output. But what is the name of this new calculated column? Well, the truth is, it has no name; it is simply a value. Although this can be fine if you are just looking at the results in a SQL query tool (for instance, MS-Query, or Microsoft SQL Server Query Analyzer), an unnamed column cannot be used within a client application because there is no way for the client to refer to that column.

To solve this problem, SQL supports column aliases. An alias is just that, an alternate name for a field or value. Aliases are assigned with the AS keyword. Take a look at the following SELECT statement:

INPUT

```
SELECT RTRIM(vend_city)+', '+RTRIM(vend_state)+'
➥'+RTRIM(vend_zip) AS address2
FROM Vendors
ORDER BY vend_name;
```

OUTPUT

```
address2
-------------------------------------------------------------
Anytown, OH 44333
Bear Town, MI 44444
Dollsville, CA 99999
New York, NY 11111
```

Here's the Oracle version:

INPUT

```
SELECT RTRIM(vend_city) || ', ' || RTRIM(vend_state) || ' ' ||
➥RTRIM(vend_zip) AS address2
FROM Vendors
ORDER BY vend_name;
```

OUTPUT

```
address2
-------------------------------------------------------------
Anytown, OH 44333
Bear Town, MI 44444
Dollsville, CA 99999
New York, NY 11111
```

ANALYSIS The SELECT statement itself is the same as the one used in the previous code snippet, except that here the calculated field is followed by the text AS address2. This instructs SQL to create a calculated field named address2 containing the calculation specified. As you can see in the output, the results are the same as before, but the column is now named address2, and any client application can refer to this column by name, just as it would to any actual table column.

> **Other Uses for Aliases** Aliases have other uses too. Some common uses include renaming a column if the real table column name contains illegal characters (for example, spaces), and expanding column names if the original names are either ambiguous or easily misread.

The complete SELECT statement to retrieve all the information for the mailing label now looks like this:

INPUT

```
SELECT vend_name,
       vend_address,
       RTRIM(vend_city)+', '+RTRIM(vend_state)+'
    ➡'+RTRIM(vend_zip) AS vend_address2
FROM Vendors
ORDER BY vend_name;
```

Here's the Oracle version:

INPUT

```
SELECT vend_name,
       vend_address,
       RTRIM(vend_city) ¦¦ ', ' ¦¦ RTRIM(vend_state) ¦¦ ' '
    ➡¦¦ RTRIM(vend_zip) AS vend_address2
FROM Vendors
ORDER BY vend_name;
```

Performing Mathematical Calculations

Another frequent use for calculated fields is performing mathematical calculations on retrieved data. Let's take a look at an example. The Orders table contains all orders received, and the OrderItems table contains the individual items within each order. The following SQL statement retrieves all the items in order number 20008:

INPUT

```
SELECT prod_id, quantity, item_price
FROM OrderItems
WHERE order_num = 20008;
```

OUTPUT

```
prod_id        quantity     item_price
----------     -----------  --------------------
RGAN01         5            4.9900
BR03           5            11.9900
BNBG01         10           3.4900
BNBG02         10           3.4900
BNBG03         10           3.4900
```

The item_price column contains the per unit price for each item in an order. To expand the item price (item price multiplied by quantity ordered), you simply do the following:

INPUT

```
SELECT prod_id,
       quantity,
       item_price,
       quantity*item_price AS expanded_price
FROM OrderItems
WHERE order_num = 20008;
```

OUTPUT

```
prod_id        quantity     item_price             expanded_price
----------     -----------  ---------------------  -------
--------------
RGAN01         5            4.9900                 24.9500
BR03           5            11.9900                59.9500
BNBG01         10           3.4900                 34.9000
BNBG02         10           3.4900                 34.9000
BNBG03         10           3.4900                 34.9000
```

ANALYSIS The expanded_price column shown in the output above is a calculated field; the calculation is simply quantity*item_price. The client application can now use this new calculated column just as it would any other column.

SQL supports the basic mathematical operators listed in Table 7.1. In addition, parentheses can be used to establish order of precedence. Refer to Lesson 5, "Advanced Data Filtering," for an explanation of precedence.

TABLE 7.1 SQL Mathematical Operators

Operator	Description
+	Addition
-	Subtraction
*	Multiplication
/	Division

Summary

In this lesson, you learned what calculated fields are and how to create them. You used examples demonstrating the use of calculated fields for both string concatenation and mathematical operations. In addition, you learned how to create and use aliases so that your application can refer to calculated fields.

LESSON 8

Using Data Manipulation Functions

In this lesson, you'll learn what functions are, what types of functions DBMSs support, and how to use these functions. You'll also learn why SQL function use can be very problematic.

Understanding Functions

Like almost any other computer language, SQL supports the use of functions to manipulate data. Functions are operations that can be performed on data, usually to facilitate conversion and manipulation.

An example of a function is the RTRIM() that we used in the last lesson to trim any spaces from the end of a string.

The Problem with Functions

Before you work through this lesson and try the examples, you should be aware that using SQL functions can be highly problematic.

Unlike SQL statements (for example, SELECT), which for the most part are supported by all DBMSs equally, functions tend to be very DBMS specific. In fact, very few functions are supported identically by all major DBMSs. Although all types of functionality are usually available in each DBMS, the function name or syntax can differ greatly. To demonstrate just how problematic this can be, Table 8.1 lists a few differences between the SQL used by two of the most popular client-server Database Management Systems—Oracle and Microsoft SQL Server.

TABLE 8.1 Function Differences Between Oracle and
Microsoft SQL Server

Function	Oracle	SQL Server
Extract part of a string	SUBSTR()	SUBSTRING()
Data type conversion	Multiple functions, one for each conversion type (for example, TO_CHAR() and TO_NUMBER())	All conversions performed using the CONVERT() function
Return a number's ceiling	CEIL()	CEILING()
Get current date	SYSDATE	GETDATE()
Get tomorrow's date	NEXT_DAY	DATEADD()

As you can see, unlike SQL statements, SQL functions are not portable.
This means that code you write for a specific SQL implementation might
not work on another implementation.

 Portable   Code that is written so that it will run on
multiple systems.

With code portability in mind, many SQL programmers opt not to use any
implementation-specific features. Although this is a somewhat noble and
idealistic view, it is not always in the best interests of application performance. If you opt not to use these functions, you make your application
code work harder. It must use other methods to do what the DBMS could
have done more efficiently.

> **Should You Use Functions?**   So now you are trying to decide whether you should or shouldn't use functions. Well, that decision is yours, and there is no right or wrong choice. If you do decide to use functions, make sure you comment your code well, so that at a later date you (or another developer) will know exactly what SQL implementation you were writing to.

Using Functions

Most SQL implementations support the following types of functions:

- Text functions are used to manipulate strings of text (for example, trimming or padding values and converting values to upper and lowercase).

- Numeric functions are used to perform mathematical operations on numeric data (for example, returning absolute numbers and performing algebraic calculations).

- Date and time functions are used to manipulate date and time values and to extract specific components from these values (for example, returning differences between dates, and checking date validity).

- System functions return information specific to the DBMS being used (for example, returning user login information).

In the last lesson, you saw a function used as part of a column list in a SELECT statement, but that's not all functions can do. You can use functions in other parts of the SELECT statement (for instance in the WHERE clause), as well as in other SQL statements (more on that in later lessons).

Text Manipulation Functions

You've already seen an example of text-manipulation functions in the last lesson—the RTRIM() function was used to trim white space from the end of a column value. Table 8.2 lists some commonly used text-manipulation functions.

TABLE 8.2 Commonly Used Text-Manipulation Functions

Function	Description
LEFT() (or use substring function)	Returns characters from left of string
LENGTH() (also DATALENGTH() or Len())	Returns the length of a string
LOWER()	Converts string to lower-case
LTRIM()	Trims white space from left of string
RIGHT() (or use substring function)	Returns characters from right of string
RTRIM()	Trims white space from right of string
SOUNDEX()	Returns a strings SOUNDEX value
UPPER()	Converts string to upper-case

One item in table 8.2 requires further explanation. SOUNDEX is an algorithm that converts any string of text into a alphanumeric pattern describing the phonetic representation of that text. SOUNDEX takes into account similar sounding characters and syllables, enabling strings to be compared by how they sound rather than how they have been typed. Although SOUNDEX is not a SQL concept, most DBMSs do offer SOUNDEX support.

Here's an example using the SOUNDEX() function. Customer Kids Place is in the Customers table and has a contact named Michelle Green. But what if that were a typo, and the contact actually was supposed to have been Michael Green? Obviously, searching by the correct contact name would return no data, as shown here:

INPUT

```
SELECT cust_name, cust_contact
FROM Customers
WHERE cust_contact = 'Michael Green' ;
```

OUTPUT

```
cust_name                            cust_contact
- - - - - - - - - - - - - - - - - - - - - - - - - - - - - - - - -    - - - - - - - - - - - - - - - - - - - - - - - - - - -
```

Now try the same search using the SOUNDEX() function to match all
contact names that sound similar to Michael Green:

INPUT

```
SELECT cust_name, cust_contact
FROM Customers
WHERE SOUNDEX(cust_contact) = SOUNDEX('Michael Green');
```

OUTPUT

```
cust_name                       cust_contact
- - - - - - - - - - - - - - - - - - - - - - - -    - - - - - - - - - - - - - - - - - - - - - - - - - - -
Kids Place                      Michelle Green
```

ANALYSIS In this example, the WHERE clause uses the SOUNDEX() function
to convert both the cust_contact column value and the search string to
their SOUNDEX values. Because Michael Green and Michelle Green sound
alike, their SOUNDEX values match, and so the WHERE clause correctly filtered the desired data.

> **Obtaining a Complete Function List** It is important
> to realize that the list in Table 8.2 is not complete.
> Feel free to experiment with any of these functions,
> but also refer to your DBMS's documentation to deter-
> mine what other text manipulation functions it
> supports.

Date and Time Manipulation Functions

Date and times are stored in tables using datatypes, and each DBMS uses
its own special varieties. Date and time values are stored in special formats so that they may be sorted or filtered quickly and efficiently, as well
as to save physical storage space.

The format used to store dates and times is usually of no use to your applications, and so date and time functions are almost always used to read, expand, and manipulate these values. Because of this, date and time manipulation functions are some of the most important functions in the SQL language. Unfortunately, they also tend to be the least consistent and least portable.

To demonstrate the use of date manipulation function, look at the following example. (These examples are presented twice, first using SQL Server functions and then using Oracle functions.)

The Orders table contains all orders along with an order date. To retrieve a list of all orders made in 1999, do the following (in Microsoft SQL Server, Sybase, and Microsoft Access):

INPUT

```
SELECT order_num
FROM Orders
WHERE DATEPART(yy, order_date) = 1999;
```

OUTPUT

```
order_num
- - - - - - - - - - -
20005
20006
20007
20008
20009
```

ANALYSIS   This example uses the SQL Server DATEPART() function which, as its name suggests, returns a part of a date. DATEPART() takes two parameters, the part to return, and the date to return it from. DATEPART(yy,order_date) returns just the year from the order_date column. By comparing that to 1999, the WHERE clause can filter just the orders for that year.

Oracle has no DATEPART() function, but there are several other date manipulation functions that can be used to accomplish the same retrieval. Here is an example:

INPUT

```
SELECT order_num
FROM Orders
WHERE to_number(to_char(order_date, 'YY')) = 1999;
```

ANALYSIS In this example, the to_char() function is used to extract part of the date, and to_number() is used to convert it to a numeric value so that it can be compared to 1999.

Another way to accomplish this same task is to use the BETWEEN operator:

INPUT

```
SELECT order_num
FROM Orders
WHERE order_date BETWEEN to_date('01-JAN-1999')
                  AND to_date('31-DEC-1999');
```

ANALYSIS In this example, Oracle's to_date() function is used to convert two strings to dates. One contains the date January 1, 1999, and the other contains the date December 31, 1999. A standard BETWEEN operator is used to find all orders between those two dates. It is worth noting that this same code would not work with SQL Server because it does not support the to_date() function. However, if you replaced to_date() with DATEPART(), you could indeed use this type of statement.

To retrieve all orders for February 1999, you filter on both the month and year, as follows (again, this is the SQL Server syntax):

INPUT

```
SELECT order_num
FROM Orders
WHERE DATEPART(yy, order_date) = 1999
      AND DATEPART(mm, order_date) = 2;
```

OUTPUT

```
order_num
- - - - - - - - - - -
20008
20009
```

ANALYSIS The WHERE clause in this example uses two DATEPART() functions, one to extract the year and one to extract the month. Both are needed. If only the month is matched, orders for February of any year are retrieved.

To accomplish this in Oracle, you can use either of the following methods:

INPUT

```
SELECT order_num
FROM Orders
WHERE to_number(to_char(order_date, 'YY')) = 1999
 AND to_number(to_char(order_date, 'MM')) = 2
```

INPUT

```
SELECT order_num
FROM Orders
WHERE order_date BETWEEN to_date('01-FEB-1999')
                 AND to_date('28-FEB-1999');
```

ANALYSIS   Just as in the previous example, the to_char() function can be used to extract specific date parts, or the Oracle to_date() function can be used to define the desired date range which is passed to a BETWEEN operator.

As you can see, date-time manipulation functions are particularly DBMS specific. Refer to your DBMS documentation for the list of the date-time manipulation functions it supports.

Numeric Manipulation Functions

Numeric manipulation functions do just that—manipulate numeric data. These functions tend to be used primarily for algebraic, trigonometric, or geometric calculations and, therefore, are not as frequently used as string or date and time manipulation functions.

The ironic thing is that of all the functions found in the major DBMSs, the numeric functions are the ones that are most uniform and consistent. Table 8.3 lists some of the more commonly used numeric manipulation functions.

TABLE 8.3 Commonly Used Numeric Manipulation Functions

Function	Description
ABS()	Returns a number's absolute value
COS()	Returns the trigonometric cosine of a specified angle
EXP()	Returns the exponential value of a specific number
PI()	Returns the value of PI
SIN()	Returns the trigonometric sine of a specified angle
SQRT()	Returns the square root of a specified number
TAN()	Returns the trigonometric tangent of a specified angle

Refer to your DBMS documentation for a list of the supported mathematical manipulation functions.

Summary

In this lesson, you learned how to use SQL's data manipulation functions. You also learned that although these functions can be extremely useful in formatting, manipulating, and filtering data, the function details are very inconsistent from one SQL implemtation to the next (as demonstrated by the differences between SQL Server and Oracle).

LESSON 9
Summarizing Data

In this lesson, you will learn what the SQL aggregate functions are and how to use them to summarize table data.

Using Aggregate Functions

It is often necessary to summarize data without actually retrieving it all, and SQL provides special functions for this purpose. Using these functions, SQL queries are often used to retrieve data for analysis and reporting purposes. Examples of this type of retrieval are

- Determining the number of rows in a table (or the number of rows that meet some condition or contain a specific value).

- Obtaining the sum of a set of rows in a table.

- Finding the highest, lowest, and average values in a table column (either for all rows or for specific rows).

In each of these examples, you want a summary of the data in a table, not the actual data itself. Therefore, returning the actual table data would be a waste of time and processing resources (not to mention bandwidth). To repeat, all you really want is the summary information.

To facilitate this type of retrieval, SQL features a set of five aggregate functions, which are listed in Table 9.1. These functions enable you to perform all the types of retrieval just enumerated. You'll be relieved to know that unlike the data manipulation functions in the last lesson, SQL's aggregate functions are supported pretty consistently by the major SQL implementations.

Aggregate Functions   Functions that operate on a set of rows to calculate and return a single value.

TABLE 9.1   SQL Aggregate Functions

Function	Description
AVG()	Returns a column's average value
COUNT()	Returns the number of rows in a column
MAX()	Returns a column's highest value
MIN()	Returns a column's lowest value
SUM()	Returns the sum of a column's values

The use of each of these functions is explained in the following sections.

The AVG() Function

AVG() is used to return the average value of a specific column by counting both the number of rows in the table and the sum of their values. AVG() can be used to return the average value of all columns or of specific columns or rows.

This first example uses AVG() to return the average price of all the products in the Products table:

INPUT

```
SELECT AVG(prod_price) AS avg_price
FROM Products;
```

OUTPUT

```
avg_price
-----------
6.0614
```

ANALYSIS   The SELECT statement above returns a single value, avg_price that contains the average price of all products in the Products table. avg_price is an alias as explained in Lesson 7, "Creating Calculated Fields."

AVG() can also be used to determine the average value of specific columns or rows. The following example returns the average price of products offered by a specific vendor:

INPUT

```
SELECT AVG(prod_price) AS avg_price
FROM Products
WHERE vend_id = 'dll01';
```

OUTPUT

```
avg_price
-----------
3.8650
```

ANALYSIS This SELECT statement differs from the previous one only in that this one contains a WHERE clause. The WHERE clause filters only products with a vendor_id of DLL01, and, therefore, the value returned in avg_price is the average of just that vendor's products.

Individual Columns Only AVG() may only be used to determine the average of a specific numeric column, and that column name must be specified as the function parameter. To obtain the average value of multiple columns, multiple AVG() functions must be used.

NULL Values Columns containing NULL values are ignored by the AVG() function.

The COUNT() Function

COUNT() does just that: It counts. Using COUNT(), you can determine the number of rows in a table or the number of rows that match a specific criteria.

COUNT() can be used two ways:

- Use COUNT(*) to count the number of rows in a table, whether columns contain values or NULL values.

- Use COUNT(column) to count the number of rows that have values in a specific column, ignoring NULL values.

This first example returns the total number of customers in the Customers table:

INPUT

```
SELECT COUNT(*) AS num_cust
FROM Customers;
```

OUTPUT

```
num_cust
--------
5
```

ANALYSIS In this example, COUNT(*) is used to count all rows, regardless of values. The count is returned in num_cust.

The following example counts just the customers with an email address:

INPUT

```
SELECT COUNT(cust_email) AS num_cust
FROM Customers;
```

INPUT

```
num_cust
--------
3
```

ANALYSIS This SELECT statement uses COUNT(cust_email) to count only rows with a value in the cust_email column. In this example, cust_email is 3 (meaning that only 3 of the 5 customers have email addresses).

 NULL Values   Columns with NULL values in them are ignored by the COUNT() function if a column name is specified, but not if the asterisk (*) is used.

The MAX() Functions

MAX() returns the highest value in a specified column. MAX() requires that the column name be specified, as seen here:

INPUT

```
SELECT MAX(prod_price) AS max_price
FROM Products;
```

OUTPUT

```
max_price
----------
11.9900
```

ANALYSIS   Here MAX() returns the price of the most expensive item in Products table.

Using MAX() With Non-Numeric Data   Although MAX() is usually used to find the highest numeric or date values, many (but not all) DBMSs allow it to be used to return the highest value in any columns including textual columns. When used with textual data, MAX() returns the row that would be the last if the data were sorted by that column.

NULL Values   Columns with NULL values in them are ignored by the MAX() function.

The MIN() Function

MIN() does the exact opposite of MAX();, it returns the lowest value in a specified column. Like MAX(), MIN() requires that the column name be specified, as seen here:

INPUT

```
SELECT MIN(prod_price) AS min_price
FROM Products;
```

OUTPUT

```
min_price
----------
3.4900
```

ANALYSIS Here MIN() returns the price of the least expensive item in Products table.

Using MIN() With Non Numeric Data Although MIN() is usually used to find the lowest numeric or date values, many (but not all) DBMSs allow it to be used to return the lowest value in any columns including textual columns. When used with textual data, MIN() will return the row that would be first if the data were sorted by that column.

NULL Values Columns with NULL values in them are ignored by the MIN() function.

The SUM() Function

SUM() is used to return the sum (total) of the values in a specific column.

Here is an example to demonstrate this. The OrderItems table contains the actual items in an order. Each item has item_price and a quantity, so the expanded price for each item is item_price*quantity (the item price multiplied by quantity orders). The total order cost is the sum of all the expanded prices in that order. Look at the following statement:

INPUT

```
SELECT SUM(item_price*quantity) AS total_price
FROM OrderItems
WHERE order_num = 20005;
```

OUTPUT

```
total_price
----------
1648.0000
```

ANALYSIS   The function SUM(item_price*quantity) returns the sum of all the expanded prices in an order, and the WHERE clause ensures that just the right order items are included.

> **Performing Calculations on Multiple Columns**   All the aggregate functions can be used to perform calculations on multiple columns using the standard mathematical operators, as shown in the example.

> **NULL Values**   Columns with NULL values in them are ignored by the SUM() function.

Aggregates on Distinct Values

The five aggregate functions can all be used in two ways:

- To perform calculations on all rows, specify the ALL argument or specify no argument at all (because ALL is the default behavior).
- To only include unique values, specify the DISTINCT argument.

> **ALL is Default**   The ALL argument need not be specified because it is the default behavior. If DISTINCT is not specified, ALL is assumed.

The following example uses the AVG() function to return the average product price offered by a specific vendor. It is the same SELECT statement used above, but here the DISTINCT argument is used so that the average only takes into account unique prices:

INPUT

```
SELECT AVG(DISTINCT prod_price) AS avg_price
FROM Products
WHERE vend_id = 'dll01';
```

OUTPUT

```
avg_price
- - - - - - - - - - -
4.2400
```

ANALYSIS As you can see, in this example avg_price is higher when DISTINCT is used because there are multiple items with the same lower price. Excluding them raises the average price.

Caution DISTINCT may only be used with COUNT() if a column name is specified. DISTINCT may not be used with COUNT(*). Similarly, DISTINCT must be used with a column name and not with a calculation or expression.

Using DISTINCT with MIN() and MAX() Although DISTINCT can actually be used with MIN() and MAX(), there is actually no value in doing so. The minimum and maximum values in a column will be the same whether or not only distinct values are included.

Additional Aggregate Arguments In addition to the DISTINCT and ALL arguments shown here, some DBMSs support additional arguments such as TOP and TOP PERCENT that let you perform calculations on subsets of query results. Refer to your DBMS documentation to determine exactly what arguments are available to you.

Combining Aggregate Functions

All the examples of aggregate function used thus far have involved a single function. But actually, SELECT statements may contain as few or as many aggregate functions as needed. Look at this example:

> **INPUT**

```
SELECT COUNT(*) AS num_items,
       MIN(prod_price) AS price_min,
       MAX(prod_price) AS price_max,
       AVG(prod_price) AS price_avg
FROM Products;
```

> **OUTPUT**

num_items	price_min	price_max	price_avg
7	3.4900	11.9900	6.0614

ANALYSIS Here a single SELECT statement performs four aggregate calculations in one step and returns four values (the number of items in the Products table, and the highest, lowest, and average product prices).

Naming Aliases When specifying alias names to contain the results of an aggregate function, try to not use the name of an actual column in the table. Although there is nothing actually illegal about doing so, many SQL implementations do not support this and will generate obscure error messages if you do so.

Summary

Aggregate functions are used to summarize data. SQL supports five aggregate functions, all of which can be used in multiple ways to return just the results you need. These functions are designed to be highly efficient, and they usually return results far more quickly than you could calculate them yourself within your own client application.

LESSON 10

Grouping Data

In this lesson, you'll learn how to group data so that you can summarize subsets of table contents. This involves two new SELECT statement clauses: the GROUP BY clause and the HAVING clause.

Understanding Data Grouping

In the last lesson, you learned that the SQL aggregate functions can be used to summarize data. This enables you to count rows, calculate sums and averages, and obtain high and low values without having to retrieve all the data.

All the calculations thus far were performed on all the data in a table or on data that matched a specific WHERE clause. As a reminder, the following example returns the number of products offered by vendor DLL01:

`INPUT`

```
SELECT COUNT(*) AS num_prods
FROM Products
WHERE vend_id = 'dll01';
```

`OUTPUT`

```
num_prods
-----------
4
```

But what if you wanted to return the number of products offered by each vendor? Or products offered by vendors who offer a single product or only those who offer more than ten products?

This is where groups come into play. Grouping lets you divide data into logical sets so that you can perform aggregate calculations on each group.

Creating Groups

Groups are created using the GROUP BY clause in your SELECT statement.
The best way to understand this is to look at an example:

INPUT

```
SELECT vend_id, COUNT(*) AS num_prods
FROM Products
GROUP BY vend_id;
```

OUTPUT

```
vend_id    num_prods
---------  ---------
BRS01      3
DLL01      4
```

ANALYSIS The above SELECT statement specifies two columns, vend_id,
which contains the ID of a product's vendor, and num_prods, which is a
calculated field (created using the COUNT(*) function). The GROUP BY
clause instructs the DBMS to sort the data and group it by vend_id. This
causes num_prods to be calculated once per vend_id rather than once for
the entire table. As you can see in the output, vendor BRS01 has 3 products
listed, and vendor DLL01 has 4 products listed.

Because you used GROUP BY, you did not have to specify each group to be
evaluated and calculated. That was done automatically. The GROUP BY
clause instructs the DBMS to group the data and then perform the aggregate on each group rather than on the entire resultset.

Before you use GROUP BY, here are some important rules about its use that
you need to know:

- GROUP BY clauses can contain as many columns as you want.
  This enables you to nest groups, providing you with more granu-
  lar control over how data is grouped.

- If you have nested groups in your GROUP BY clause, data is summarized at the last specified group. In other words, all the
  columns specified are evaluated together when grouping is established (so you won't get data back for each individual column
  level).

- Every column listed in GROUP BY must be a retrieved column or a valid expression (but not an aggregate function). If an expression is used in the SELECT, that same expression must be specified in GROUP BY. Aliases cannot be used.

- Most SQL implementations do not allow GROUP BY columns with variable length datatypes (such as text or memo fields).

- Aside from the aggregate calculations statements, every column in your SELECT statement must be present in the GROUP BY clause.

- If the grouping column contains a row with a NULL value, NULL will be returned as a group. If there are multiple rows with NULL values, they'll all be grouped together.

- The GROUP BY clause must come after any WHERE clause and before any ORDER BY clause.

The ALL Clause Some SQL implementations (such as Microsoft SQL Server) support an optional ALL clause within GROUP BY. This clause can be used to return all groups, even those that have no matching rows. (In that case, the aggregate would return NULL.) Refer to your DBMS documentation to see if it supports ALL.

Specifying Columns by Relative Position Some SQL implementations allow you to specify GROUP BY columns by the position in the SELECT list. For example, GROUP BY 2,1 can mean group by the second column selected and then by the first. Although this shorthand syntax is convenient, it is not supported by all SQL implementations. Refer to your DBMS documentation for more information on this.

Filtering Groups

In addition to being able to group data using GROUP BY, SQL also allows you to filter which groups to include and which to exclude. For example, you might want a list of all customers who have made at least two orders. To get this, you must filter based on the complete group, not on individual rows.

You've already seen the WHERE clause in action (that was introduced back in Lesson 4, "Filtering Data." But WHERE does not work here because WHERE filters specific rows, not groups. As a matter of fact, WHERE has no idea what a group is.

So what do you use instead of WHERE? SQL provides yet another clause for this purpose: the HAVING clause. HAVING is very similar to WHERE. In fact, all types of WHERE clauses you learned about thus far can also be used with HAVING. The only difference is that WHERE filters rows and HAVING filters groups.

> **HAVING Supports All Of WHERE's Operators**   In Lesson 4 and Lesson 5, "Advanced Data Filtering," you learned about WHERE clause conditions (including wildcard conditions and clauses with multiple operators). All the techniques and options that you learned about WHERE can be applied to HAVING. The syntax is identical; just the keyword changes.

So how do you filter rows? Look at the following example:

INPUT

```
SELECT cust_id, COUNT(*) AS orders
FROM Orders
GROUP BY cust_id
HAVING COUNT(*) >= 2;
```

OUTPUT

```
cust_id      orders
----------   ----------
1000000001   2
```

ANALYSIS The first three lines of this SELECT statement are similar to the statements seen above. The final line adds a HAVING clause that filters on those groups with a COUNT(*) >= 2—two or more orders.

As you can see, a WHERE clause does not work here because the filtering is based on the group aggregate value, not on the values of specific rows.

So is there ever a need to use both WHERE and HAVING clauses in one statement? Actually, yes, there is. Suppose you want to further filter the above statement so that it returns any customers who placed two or more orders in the past twelve months. To do that, you can add a WHERE clause that filters out just the orders placed in the past twelve months. You then add a HAVING clause to filter just the groups with two or more rows in them.

> **Using HAVING and WHERE** HAVING is so similar to WHERE that most DBMSs treat them as the same thing if no GROUP BY is specified. Nevertheless, you should make that distinction yourself. Use HAVING only in conjunction with GROUP BY clauses. Use WHERE for standard row-level filtering.

Grouping and Sorting

It is important to understand that GROUP BY and ORDER BY are very different, even though they often accomplish the same thing. Table 10.1 summarizes the differences between them.

TABLE 10.1 ORDER BY Versus GROUP BY

ORDER BY	GROUP BY
Sorts generated output	Groups rows. The output might not be in group order, however.
Any columns (even columns not selected) or may be used	Only selected columns or expressions or may be used, and every selected column expression must be used.
Never required	Required if using columns (or expressions) with aggregate functions.

The first difference listed in Table 10.1 is extremely important. More often than not, you will find that data grouped using GROUP BY will indeed be output in group order. But that is not always the case, and it is not actually required by the SQL specifications. Furthermore, even if your particular DBMS does, in fact, always sort the data by the specified GROUP BY clause, you might actually want it sorted differently. Just because you group data one way (to obtain group specific aggregate values) does not mean that you want the output sorted that same way. You should always provide an explicit ORDER BY clause as well, even if it is identical to the GROUP BY clause.

> **Don't Forget ORDER BY**   As a rule, anytime you use a GROUP BY clause, you should also specify an ORDER BY clause. That is the only way to ensure that data will be sorted properly. Never rely on GROUP BY to sort your data.

To demonstrate the use of both GROUP BY and ORDER BY, let's look at an example. The following SELECT statement is similar to the ones seen previously. It retrieves the order number and number of items ordered for all orders containing three or more items:

INPUT

```
SELECT order_num, COUNT(*) AS items
FROM OrderItems
GROUP BY order_num
HAVING COUNT(*) >= 3;
```

OUTPUT

```
order_num    items
----------   -----
20006        3
20007        5
20008        5
20009        3
```

To sort the output by number of items ordered, all you need to do is add
an ORDER BY clause, as follows:

INPUT

```
SELECT order_num, COUNT(*) AS items
FROM OrderItems
GROUP BY order_num
HAVING COUNT(*) >= 3
ORDER BY items, order_num;
```

OUTPUT

```
order_num    items
----------   -----
20006        3
20009        3
20007        5
20008        5
```

ANALYSIS In this example, the GROUP BY clause is used to group the data
by order number (the order_num column) so that the COUNT(*) function
can return the number of items in each order. The HAVING clause filters the
data so that only orders with three or more items are returned. Finally, the
output is sorted using the ORDER BY clause.

SELECT Clause Ordering

This is probably a good time to review the order in which SELECT statement clauses are to be specified. Table 10.2 lists all the clauses we have
learned thus far, in the order they must be used.

TABLE 10.2 SELECT Clauses and Their Sequence

Clause	Description	Required
SELECT	Columns or expressions to be returned	Yes
FROM	Table to retrieve data from	Only if selecting from a table
WHERE	Row-level filtering	No

continues

TABLE 10.2 Continued

Clause	Description	Required
GROUP BY	Group specification	Only if calculating aggregates by group
HAVING	Group-level filtering	No
ORDER BY	Output sort order	No

Summary

In Lesson 9, "Summarizing Data," you learned how to use the SQL aggregate functions to perform summary calculations on your data. In this lesson, you learned how to use the GROUP BY clause to perform these calculations on groups of data, returning results for each group. You saw how to use the HAVING clause to filter specific groups. You also learned the difference between ORDER BY and GROUP BY and between WHERE and HAVING.

LESSON 11

Working with Subqueries

In this lesson, you'll learn what subqueries are and how to use them.

Understanding Subqueries

SELECT statements are SQL queries. All the SELECT statements we have seen thus far are simple queries: single statements retrieving data from individual database tables.

 Query   Any SQL statement. However, the term is usually used to refer to SELECT statements.

SQL also enables you to create *subqueries*: queries that are embedded into other queries. Why would you want to do this? The best way to understand this concept is to look at a couple of examples.

Filtering by Subquery

The database tables used in all the lessons in this book are relational tables. (See Appendix A, "Sample Table Scripts," for a description of each of the tables and their relationships.) Orders are stored in two tables. The Orders table stores a single row for each order containing order number, customer ID, and order date. The individual order items are stored in the related OrderItems table. The Orders table does not store customer information. It only stores a customer ID. The actual customer information is stored in the Customers table.

Now suppose you wanted a list of all the customers who ordered item
RGAN01. What would you have to do to retrieve this information? Here are
the steps:

1. Retrieve the order numbers of all orders containing item RGAN01.

2. Retrieve the customer ID of all the customers who have orders
   listed in the order numbers returned in the previous step.

3. Retrieve the customer information for all the customer IDs
   returned in the previous step.

Each of these steps can be executed as a separate query. By doing so, you
use the results returned by one SELECT statement to populate the WHERE
clause of the next SELECT statement.

You can also use subqueries to combine all three queries into one single
statement.

The first SELECT statement should be self-explanatory by now. It retrieves
the order_num column for all order items with a prod_id of RGAN01. The
output lists the two orders containing this item:

INPUT

```
SELECT order_num
FROM OrderItems
WHERE prod_id = 'RGAN01';
```

OUTPUT

```
order_num
-----------
20007
20008
```

The next step is to retrieve the customer IDs associated with orders 20007
and 20008. Using the IN clause described in Lesson 5, "Advanced Data
Filtering," you can create a SELECT statement as follows:

INPUT

```
SELECT cust_id
FROM Orders
WHERE order_num IN (20007,20008);
```

OUTPUT

```
cust_id
----------
1000000004
1000000005
```

Now, combine the two queries by turning the first (the one that returned the order numbers) into a subquery. Look at the following SELECT statement:

INPUT

```
SELECT cust_id
FROM Orders
WHERE order_num IN (SELECT order_num
                    FROM OrderItems
                    WHERE prod_id = 'RGAN01');
```

OUTPUT

```
cust_id
----------
1000000004
1000000005
```

ANALYSIS Subqueries are always processed starting with the innermost SELECT statement and working outward. When the preceding SELECT statement is processed, the DBMS actually performs two operations.

First it runs the subquery:

```
SELECT order_num FROM orderitems WHERE prod_id='RGAN01'
```

That query returns the two order numbers 20007 and 20008. Those two values are then passed to the WHERE clause of the outer query in the comma-delimited format required by the IN operator. The outer query now becomes

```
SELECT cust_id FROM orders WHERE order_num IN (20007,20008)
```

As you can see, the output is correct and exactly the same as the output returned by the hard-coded WHERE clause above.

> **Formatting Your SQL**   SELECT statements containing subqueries can be difficult to read and debug, especially as they grow in complexity. Breaking up the queries over multiple lines and indenting the lines appropriately as shown here can greatly simplify working with subqueries.

You now have the IDs of all the customers who ordered item RGAN01. The next step is to retrieve the customer information for each of those customer IDs. The SQL statement to retrieve the two columns is

INPUT

```
SELECT cust_name, cust_contact
FROM Customers
WHERE cust_id IN ('1000000004','1000000005');
```

Instead of hard-coding those customer IDs, you can turn this WHERE clause into a subquery:

INPUT

```
SELECT cust_name, cust_contact
FROM Customers
WHERE cust_id IN (SELECT cust_id
                  FROM Orders
                  WHERE order_num IN (SELECT order_num
                                      FROM OrderItems
                                      WHERE prod_id = 'RGAN01'));
```

OUTPUT

```
cust_name                           cust_contact
--------------------------------    --------------------
Fun4All                             Denise L. Stephens
The Toy Store                       Kim Howard
```

ANALYSIS   To execute the above SELECT statement, the DBMS had to actually perform three SELECT statements. The innermost subquery returned a list of order numbers that were then used as the WHERE clause for the subquery above it. That subquery returned a list of customer IDs that were used as the WHERE clause for the top-level query. The top-level query actually returned the desired data.

As you can see, using subqueries in a WHERE clause enables you to write extremely powerful and flexible SQL statements. There is no limit imposed on the number of subqueries that can be nested, although in practice you will find that performance will tell you when you are nesting too deeply.

> **Single Column Only**   Subquery SELECT statements can only retrieve a single column. Attempting to retrieve multiple columns will return an error.

> **Subqueries and Performance**   The code shown here works, and it achieves the desired result. Using subqueries is not always, however, the most efficient way to perform this type of data retrieval. More on this in Lesson 12, "Joining Tables," where you will revisit this same example.

Using Subqueries as Calculated Fields

Another way to use subqueries is in creating calculated fields. Suppose you wanted to display the total number of orders placed by every customer in your Customers table. Orders are stored in the Orders table along with the appropriate customer ID.

To perform this operation, follow these steps:

1. Retrieve the list of customers from the Customers table.

2. For each customer retrieved, count the number of associated orders in the Orders table.

As you learned in the previous two lessons, you can use SELECT COUNT(*) to count rows in a table, and by providing a WHERE clause to filter a specific customer ID, you can count just that customer's orders. For example, the following code counts the number of orders placed by customer 1000000001:

INPUT

```
SELECT COUNT(*) AS orders
FROM Orders
WHERE cust_id = '1000000001';
```

To perform that COUNT(*) calculation for each customer, use COUNT* as a subquery. Look at the following code:

INPUT

```
SELECT cust_name,
       cust_state,
       (SELECT COUNT(*)
        FROM Orders
        WHERE Orders.cust_id = Customers.cust_id) AS orders
FROM Customers
ORDER BY cust_name;
```

OUTPUT

```
cust_name                     cust_state        orders
------------------------       ----------        ------
Fun4All                        IN                1
Fun4All                        AZ                1
Kids Place                     OH                0
The Toy Store                  IL                1
Village Toys                   MI                2
```

ANALYSIS   This SELECT statement returns three columns for every customer in the Customers table, cust_name, cust_state, and orders. Orders is a calculated field that is set by a subquery that is provided in parentheses. That subquery is executed once for every customer retrieved. In the example above, the subquery is executed five times because five customers were retrieved.

The WHERE clause in the subquery is a little different from the WHERE clauses used previously because it uses fully qualified column names. The following clause tells SQL to compare the cust_id in the Orders table to the one currently being retrieved from the Customers table:

```
WHERE Orders.cust_id = Customers.cust_id
```

This syntax—the table name and the column name separated by a period—must be used whenever there is possible ambiguity about column names. In this example, there are two cust_id columns, one in Customers and one in Orders. Without fully qualifying the column names, the

DBMS assumes you are comparing the cust_id in the Orders table to itself. Because

```
SELECT COUNT(*) FROM Orders WHERE cust_id = cust_id
```

will always return the total number of orders in the Orders table, the results will not be what you expected:

INPUT

```
SELECT cust_name,
       cust_state,
       (SELECT COUNT(*)
        FROM Orders
        WHERE cust_id = cust_id) AS orders
FROM Customers
ORDER BY cust_name;
```

OUTPUT

cust_name	cust_state	orders
Fun4All	IN	5
Fun4All	AZ	5
Kids Place	OH	5
The Toy Store	IL	5
Village Toys	MI	5

Although subqueries are extremely useful in constructing this type of SELECT statement, care must be taken to properly qualify ambiguous column names.

Tip As explained earlier in this lesson, although the sample code shown here works, it is often not the most efficient way to perform this type of data retrieval. You will revisit this example in a later lesson.

Summary

In this lesson, you learned what subqueries are and how to use them. The most common uses for subqueries are in WHERE clause IN operators and for populating calculated columns. You saw examples of both of these types of operations.

LESSON 12
Joining Tables

In this lesson, you'll learn what joins are, why they are used, and how to create SELECT *statements using them.*

Understanding Joins

One of SQL's most powerful features is the capability to join tables on-the-fly within data retrieval queries. Joins are one of the most important operations that you can perform using SQL SELECT, and a good understanding of joins and join syntax is an extremely important part of learning SQL.

But before you can effectively use joins, you must understand relational tables and the basics of relational database design. What follows is by no means complete coverage of the subject, but it should be enough to get you up and running.

Understanding Relational Tables

The best way to understand relational tables is to look at a real-world example.

Suppose you had a database table containing a product catalog, with each catalog item in its own row. The kind of information you would store with each item would include a product description and price, along with vendor information about the company that creates the product.

Now suppose that you had multiple catalog items created by the same vendor. Where would you store the vendor information (things like vendor name, address, and contact information)? You wouldn't want to store that data along with the products for several reasons:

- Because the vendor information is the same for each product that vendor produces, repeating the information for each product is a waste of time and storage space.

- If vendor information changes (for example, if the vendor moves or his area code changes), you are required to update every occurrence of vendor information.

- When data is repeated, (that is, the vendor information is used with each product), there is a high likelihood that the data will not be entered exactly the same way each time. Inconsistent data is extremely difficult to use in reporting.

The key here is that having multiple occurrences of the same data is never a good thing, and that principle is the basis for relational database design. Relational tables are designed so that information is split into multiple tables, one for each data type. The tables are related to each other through common values (and thus the *relational* in relational design).

In our example, you can create two tables, one for vendor information and one for product information. The vendors table contains all the vendor information, one table row per vendor, along with a unique identifier for each vendor. This value, called a *primary key*, can be a vendor ID, or any other unique value.

 Primary Key A column (or columns) in a table whose values uniquely identify each row in the table.

The products table stores only product information, and no vendor specific information other than the vendor ID (the vendors table's primary key). This key relates the vendors table to the products table, and using this vendor ID enables you to use the vendors table to find the details about the appropriate vendor.

What does this do for you? Well, consider the following:

- Vendor information is never repeated, and so time and space are not wasted.

- If vendor information changes, you can update a single record, the one in the vendors table. Data in related tables does not change.

- As no data is repeated, the data used is obviously consistent, making data reporting and manipulation much simpler.

The bottom line is that relational data can be stored efficiently and manipulated easily. Because of this, relational databases scale far better than nonrelational databases.

> **Scale**   Able to handle an increasing load without failing. A well-designed database or application is said to scale well.

Why Use Joins

As just explained, breaking data into multiple tables enables more efficient storage, easier manipulation, and greater scalability. But these benefits comes with a price.

If data is stored in multiple tables, how can you retrieve that data with a single SELECT statement?

The answer is to use a join. Simply put, a join is a mechanism used to associate tables within a SELECT statement (and thus the name join). Using a special syntax, multiple tables can be joined so that a single set of output is returned, and the join associates the correct rows in each table on-the-fly.

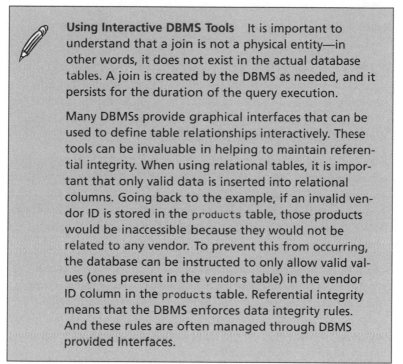

Using Interactive DBMS Tools   It is important to understand that a join is not a physical entity—in other words, it does not exist in the actual database tables. A join is created by the DBMS as needed, and it persists for the duration of the query execution.

Many DBMSs provide graphical interfaces that can be used to define table relationships interactively. These tools can be invaluable in helping to maintain referential integrity. When using relational tables, it is important that only valid data is inserted into relational columns. Going back to the example, if an invalid vendor ID is stored in the products table, those products would be inaccessible because they would not be related to any vendor. To prevent this from occurring, the database can be instructed to only allow valid values (ones present in the vendors table) in the vendor ID column in the products table. Referential integrity means that the DBMS enforces data integrity rules. And these rules are often managed through DBMS provided interfaces.

Creating a Join

Creating a join is very simple. You must specify all the tables to include and how they are related to each other. Look at the following example:

INPUT

```
SELECT vend_name, prod_name, prod_price
FROM Vendors, Products
WHERE vendors.vend_id = products.vend_id;
```

OUTPUT

```
vend_name                prod_name               prod_price
- - - - - - - - - - - -   - - - - - - - - - - - - - - - - -
Doll House Inc.          Fish bean bag toy       3.4900
Doll House Inc.          Bird bean bag toy       3.4900
Doll House Inc.          Rabbit bean bag toy     3.4900
Bears R Us               8 inch teddy bear       5.9900
```

```
Bears R Us              12 inch teddy bear    8.9900
Bears R Us              18 inch teddy bear    11.9900
Doll House Inc.         Raggedy Ann           4.9900
```

ANALYSIS   Let's take a look at the preceding code. The SELECT statement
starts in the same way as all the statements you've look at thus far, by
specifying the columns to be retrieved. The big difference here is that two
of the specified columns (prod_name and prod_price) are in one table,
whereas the other (vend_name) is in another table.

Now look at the FROM clause. Unlike all the prior SELECT statements, this
one has two tables listed in the FROM clause, vendors and products. These
are the names of the two tables that are being joined in this SELECT statement. The tables are correctly joined with a WHERE clause that instructs the
DBMS to match vend_id in the vendors table with vend_id in the
products table.

You'll notice that the columns are specified as vendors.vend_id and
products.vend_id. This fully qualified column name is required here
because if you just specified vend_id, the DBMS cannot tell which
vend_id columns you are referring to. (There are two of them, one in each
table.) As you can see in the preceding output, a single SELECT statement
returns data from two different tables.

> **Fully Qualifying Column Names**   You must use the
> fully qualified column name (table and column sepa-
> rated by a period) whenever there is a possible ambi-
> guity about which column you are referring to. Most
> DBMSs will return an error message if you refer to an
> ambiguous column name without fully qualifying it
> with a table name.

The Importance of the WHERE Clause

It might seem strange to use a WHERE clause to set the join relationship,
but actually, there is a very good reason for this. Remember, when tables
are joined in a SELECT statement, that relationship is constructed
on-the-fly. There is nothing in the database table definitions that can

instruct the DBMS how to join the tables. You have to do that yourself. When you join two tables, what you are actually doing is pairing every row in the first table with every row in the second table. The WHERE clause (as all WHERE clauses) acts as a filter to only include rows that match the specified filter condition—here the join condition.

Cartesian Product   The results returned by a table relationship without a join condition. The number of rows retrieved will be the number of rows in the first table multiplied by the number of rows in the second table.

To understand this, look at the following SELECT statement and output:

INPUT

```
SELECT vend_name, prod_name, prod_price
FROM Vendors, Products;
```

OUTPUT

```
vend_name             prod_name              prod_price
--------------------  ---------------------  ----------
Bear Emporium         Fish bean bag toy      3.4900
Bear Emporium         Bird bean bag toy      3.4900
Bear Emporium         Rabbit bean bag toy    3.4900
Bear Emporium         8 inch teddy bear      5.9900
Bear Emporium         12 inch teddy bear     8.9900
Bear Emporium         18 inch teddy bear     11.9900
Bear Emporium         Raggedy Ann            4.9900
Bears R Us            Fish bean bag toy      3.4900
Bears R Us            Bird bean bag toy      3.4900
Bears R Us            Rabbit bean bag toy    3.4900
Bears R Us            8 inch teddy bear      5.9900
Bears R Us            12 inch teddy bear     8.9900
Bears R Us            18 inch teddy bear     11.9900
Bears R Us            Raggedy Ann            4.9900
Doll House Inc.       Fish bean bag toy      3.4900
Doll House Inc.       Bird bean bag toy      3.4900
Doll House Inc.       Rabbit bean bag toy    3.4900
Doll House Inc.       8 inch teddy bear      5.9900
Doll House Inc.       12 inch teddy bear     8.9900
Doll House Inc.       18 inch teddy bear     11.9900
```

Doll House Inc.	Raggedy Ann	4.9900
Furball Inc.	Fish bean bag toy	3.4900
Furball Inc.	Bird bean bag toy	3.4900
Furball Inc.	Rabbit bean bag toy	3.4900
Furball Inc.	8 inch teddy bear	5.9900
Furball Inc.	12 inch teddy bear	8.9900
Furball Inc.	18 inch teddy bear	11.9900
Furball Inc.	Raggedy Ann	4.9900

ANALYSIS As you can see in the preceding output, the Cartesian Product is seldom what you want. The data returned here has matched every product with every vendor, including products with the incorrect vendor.

Don't Forget the WHERE Clause Make sure all your joins have WHERE clauses, or the DBMS will return far more data than you want. Similarly, make sure your WHERE clauses are correct. An incorrect filter condition will cause the DBMS to return incorrect data.

CROSS JOINS Sometimes you'll hear the type of join that returns a Cartesian Product referred to as a CROSS JOIN.

Inner Joins

The join you have been using so far is called an EQUIJOIN—a join based on the testing of equality between two tables. This kind of join is also called an INNER JOIN. In fact, some DBMSs use a slightly different syntax for these joins specifying the type of join explicitly. The following SELECT statement returns the exact same data as the preceding example (this will not work with Oracle):

INPUT

```
SELECT vend_name, prod_name, prod_price
FROM Vendors INNER JOIN Products
 ON vendors.vend_id = products.vend_id;
```

ANALYSIS The SELECT in the statement is the same as the preceding SELECT statement, but the FROM clause is different. Here the relationship between the two tables is part of the FROM clause specified as INNER JOIN. When using this syntax the join condition is specified using the special ON clause instead of a WHERE clause. The actual condition passed to ON is the same as would be passed to WHERE.

Refer to your DBMS documentation to see which syntax is preferred.

Joining Multiple Tables

SQL imposes no limit to the number of tables that may be joined in a SELECT statement. The basic rules for creating the join remain the same. First list all the tables, and then define the relationship between each. Here is an example:

INPUT

```
SELECT prod_name, vend_name, prod_price, quantity
FROM OrderItems, Products, Vendors
WHERE Products.vend_id = Vendors.vend_id
 AND OrderItems.prod_id = Products.prod_id
 AND order_num = 20007;
```

OUTPUT

```
prod_name            vend_name          prod_price   quantity
--------------       --------------     ----------   --------
18 inch teddy bear   Bears R Us         11.9900      50
Fish bean bag toy    Doll House Inc.    3.4900       100
Bird bean bag toy    Doll House Inc.    3.4900       100
Rabbit bean bag toy  Doll House Inc.    3.4900       100
Raggedy Ann          Doll House Inc.    4.9900       50
```

ANALYSIS This example displays the items in order number 20007. Order items are stored in the OrderItems table. Each product is stored by its product ID, which refers to a product in the Products table. The products are linked to the appropriate vendor in the vendors table by the vendor

ID, which is stored with each product record. The FROM clause here lists the three tables, and the WHERE clause defines both of those join conditions. An additional WHERE condition is then used to filter just the items for order 20007.

 Performance Considerations DBMSs processes joins at run-time relating each table as specified. This process can become very resource intensive so be careful not to join tables unnecessarily. The more tables you join the more performance will degrade.

 Maximum Number of Tables in a Join While it is true that SQL itself has no maximum number of tables per join restriction, many DBMSs do indeed have restrictions. Refer to your DBMS documentation to determine what restrictions there are, if any.

Now would be a good time to revisit the following example from Lesson 11, "Working with Subqueries." As you will recall, this SELECT statement returns a list of customers who ordered product RGAN01:

INPUT

```
SELECT cust_name, cust_contact
FROM Customers
WHERE cust_id IN (SELECT cust_id
                  FROM Orders
                  WHERE order_num IN (SELECT order_num
                                      FROM OrderItems
                                      WHERE prod_id = 'RGAN01'));
```

As I mentioned in Lesson 11, subqueries are not always the most efficient way to perform complex SELECT operations, and so as promised, here is the same query using joins:

INPUT

```
SELECT cust_name, cust_contact
FROM Customers, Orders, OrderItems
WHERE Customers.cust_id = Orders.cust_id
 AND OrderItems.order_num = Orders.order_num
 AND prod_id = 'RGAN01';
```

OUTPUT

```
cust_name                            cust_contact
---------------------------          --------------------
Fun4All                              Denise L. Stephens
The Toy Store                        Kim Howard
```

ANALYSIS As explained in Lesson 11, returning the data needed in this query requires the use of three tables. But instead of using them within nested subqueries, here two joins are used to connect the tables. There are three WHERE clause conditions here. The first two connect the tables in the join, and the last one filters the data for product RGAN01.

> **It Pays to Experiment** As you can see, there is often more than one way to perform any given SQL operation. And there is rarely an definitive right or wrong way. Performance can be affected by the type of operation, the DBMS being used, the amount of data in the tables, whether or not indexes and keys are present, and a whole slew of other criteria. Therefore, it is often worth experimenting with different selection mechanisms to find the one that works best for you.

Summary

Joins are one of the most important and powerful features in SQL, and using them effectively requires a basic understanding of relational database design. In this lesson, you learned some of the basics of relational database design as an introduction to learning about joins. You also learned how to create an EQUIJOIN (also known as an INNER JOIN, which is the most commonly used form of join. In the next, lesson, you'll learn how to create other types of joins.

Creating Advanced Joins

In this lesson, you'll learn all about additional join types—what they are, and how to use them. You'll also learn how to use table aliases and how to use aggregate functions with joined tables.

Using Table Aliases

Back in Lesson 7, "Creating Calculated Fields," you learned how to use aliases to refer to retrieved table columns. The syntax to alias a column looks like this:

SYNTAX

```
SELECT RTRIM(vend_city)+', '+RTRIM(vend_state)+'
'+RTRIM(vend_zip) AS address2
FROM Vendors
ORDER BY vend_name;
```

In addition to using aliases for column names and calculated fields, SQL also enables you to alias table names. There are two primary reasons to do this:

- To shorten the SQL syntax

- To enable multiple uses of the same table within a single SELECT statement

Take a look at the following SELECT statement. It is basically the same statement as an example used in the previous lesson, but it has been modified to use aliases:

```
SELECT cust_name, cust_contact
FROM Customers AS C, Orders AS O, OrderItems AS OI
WHERE C.cust_id = O.cust_id
 AND OI.order_num = O.order_num
 AND prod_id = 'RGAN01';
```

ANALYSIS You'll notice that the three tables in the FROM clauses all have aliases. Customers AS C establishes C as an alias for Customers, and so on. This enables you to use the abbreviated C instead of the full text Customers. In this example, the table aliases were used only in the WHERE clause, but aliases are not limited to just WHERE. You can use aliases in the SELECT list, the ORDER BY clause, and in any other part of the statement as well.

It is worth noting that some DBMSs (most notably Oracle) support table aliases without the use of the AS keyword. The following is the Oracle syntax for the above SELECT statement:

```
SELECT cust name, cust contact
FROM Customers C, Orders O, OrderItems OI
WHERE C.cust_id = O.cust_id
 AND OI.order_num = O.order_num
 AND prod_id = 'RGAN01';
```

 **Use of AS** Some SQL implementations (such as Oracle) do not support the AS keyword. These DBMSs still support the use of aliases but without the AS. Instead, you simply specify the alias name right after the table name. The DBMS then knows that it's an alias (Customers C instead of Customers AS C). Refer to your DBMS documentation for more information.

It is worth noting that table aliases are only used during query execution. Unlike column aliases, table aliases are never returned to the client.

Join Types

So far, you have used only simple joins known as inner joins or equijoins. You'll now take a look at three additional join types: the self join, the natural join, and the outer join.

Creating Self-Joins

As I mentioned earlier, one of the primary reasons to use table aliases is to be able to refer to the same table more than once in a single SELECT statement. An example will demonstrate this.

Suppose you wanted to send a mailing to all the customer contacts who work for the same company for which Jim Jones works. This query requires that you first find out which company Jim Jones works for, and next which customers work for that company. The following is one way to approach this problem:

INPUT

```
SELECT cust_id, cust_name, cust_contact
FROM Customers
WHERE cust_name = (SELECT cust_name
                   FROM Customers
                   WHERE cust_contact = 'Jim Jones');
```

OUTPUT

```
cust_id                 cust_name             cust_contact
--------                --------------        --------------
1000000003              Fun4All               Jim Jones
1000000004              Fun4All               Denise L. Stephens
```

ANALYSIS This first solution uses subqueries. The inner SELECT statement does a simple retrieval to return the cust_name of the company that Jim Jones works for. That name is the one used in the WHERE clause of the outer query so that all employees who work for that company are retrieved. (You learned all about subqueries in Lesson 11. Refer to that lesson for more information.)

Now look at the same query using a join:

INPUT

```
SELECT c1.cust_id, c1.cust_name, c1.cust_contact
FROM Customers AS c1, Customers AS c2
WHERE c1.cust_name = c2.cust_name
  AND c2.cust_contact = 'Jim Jones';
```

OUTPUT

cust_id	cust_name	cust_contact
1000000003	Fun4All	Jim Jones
1000000004	Fun4All	Denise L. Stephens

Here is the Oracle version of this statement:

INPUT

```
SELECT c1.cust_id, c1.cust_name, c1.cust_contact
FROM Customers c1, Customers c2
WHERE c1.cust_name = c2.cust_name
  AND c2.cust_contact = 'Jim Jones';
```

ANALYSIS   The two tables needed in this query are actually the same table, and so the Customers table appears in the FROM clause twice. Although this is perfectly legal, any references to table Customers would be ambiguous because the DBMS does not know which Customers table you are referring to.

To resolve this problem table aliases are used. The first occurrence of Customers has an alias of C1, and the second has an alias of C2. Now those aliases can be used as table names. The SELECT statement, for example, uses the C1 prefix to explicitly state the full name of the desired columns. If it did not, the DBMS would return an error because there are two columns named cust_id, cust_name, and cust_contact. It cannot know which one you want (even though, in truth, they are one and the same). The WHERE clause first joins the tables, and then it filters the data by cust_contact in the second table to return only the desired data.

> **Self Joins Instead of Subqueries**   Self joins are often used to replace statements using subqueries that retrieve data from the same table as the outer statement. Although the end result is the same, many DBMSs process joins far more quickly than they do subqueries. It is usually worth experimenting with both to determine which performs better.

Natural Joins

Whenever tables are joined, at least one column will appear in more than one table (the columns being joined). Standard joins (the inner joins that you learned about in the last lesson) return all data, even multiple occurrences of the same column. A natural join simply eliminates those multiple occurrences so that only one of each column is returned.

How does it do this? The answer is it doesn't—you do it. A natural join is a join in which you select only columns that are unique. This is typically done using a wildcard (SELECT *) for one table and explicit subsets of the columns for all other tables. The following is an example:

INPUT
```
SELECT C.*, O.order_num, O.order_date, OI.prod_id, OI.
quantity, OI.item_price
FROM Customers AS C, Orders AS O, OrderItems AS OI
WHERE C.cust_id = O.cust_id
 AND OI.order_num = O.order_num
 AND prod_id = 'RGAN01';
```

Oracle users should use the following syntax (minus the AS keyword used above):

INPUT
```
SELECT C.*, O.order_num, O.order_date, OI.prod_id, OI.
quantity, OI.item_price
FROM Customers C, Orders O, OrderItems OI
WHERE C.cust_id = O.cust_id
 AND OI.order_num = O.order_num
 AND prod_id = 'RGAN01';
```

ANALYSIS In this example, a wildcard is used for the first table only. All other columns are explicitly listed so that no duplicate columns are retrieved.

The truth is, every inner join you have created thus far is actually a natural join, and you will probably never even need an inner join that is not a natural join.

Outer Joins

Most joins relate rows in one table with rows in another. But occasionally, you will want to include rows that have no related rows. For example, you might use joins to accomplish the following tasks:

- Count how many orders were placed by each customer, including customers that have yet to place an order
- List all products with order quantities, including products not ordered by anyone
- Calculate average sale sizes, taking into account customers that have not yet placed an order

In each of these examples, the join includes table rows that have no associated rows in the related table. This type of join is called an outer join.

> **Syntax Differences** It is important to note that the syntax used to create an outer join can vary slightly among different SQL implementations. The various forms of syntax described in the following section cover most implementations, but refer to your DBMS documentation to verify its syntax before proceeding.

The following SELECT statement is a simple inner join. It retrieves a list of all customers and their orders:

INPUT

```
SELECT Customers.cust_id, Orders.order_num
FROM Customers, Orders
WHERE Customers.cust_id = Orders.cust_id;
```

To retrieve a list of all customers, including those who have placed no orders, you can do the following:

INPUT

```
SELECT Customers.cust_id, Orders.order_num
FROM Customers, Orders
WHERE Customers.cust_id *= Orders.cust_id;
```

OUTPUT

```
cust_id           order_num
----------        ---------
1000000001        20005
1000000001        20009
1000000002        NULL
1000000003        20006
1000000004        20007
1000000005        20008
```

ANALYSIS   The only difference between this SELECT statement and the previous one is the operator in the WHERE clause. Instead of testing for equality with a =, the *= operator is used to specify that every row in the Customers table should be included. *= is the left outer join operator. It retrieves all the rows from the left table.

The opposite of the left outer join is the right outer join specified by the =* operator. It can be used to return all rows from the table listed to the right of the operator, as seen in this next example:

INPUT

```
SELECT Customers.cust_id, Orders.order_num
FROM Customers, Orders
WHERE Orders.cust_id =* Customers.cust_id;
```

As explained in the last lesson, some DBMSs require the use of a slightly different join syntax. The following example of the same SELECT statement uses explicit OUTER JOIN syntax instead of a WHERE clause operator. The end result is the same, however.

```
SELECT Customers.cust_id, Orders.order_num
FROM Customers LEFT OUTER JOIN Orders
 ON Customers.cust_id = Orders.cust_id;
```

ANALYSIS Like the inner join seen in the last lesson, this SELECT statement uses the keywords OUTER JOIN to specify the join type (instead of specifying it in the WHERE clause). But unlike inner joins, which relate rows in both tables, outer joins also include rows with no related rows. And as seen in the preceding example, when creating an outer join, you must specify the table from which you wish to include all the rows. In the previous examples, you used *- and -* for this. When using OUTER JOIN syntax, however, you must use the RIGHT or LEFT keywords. The previous example uses LEFT OUTER JOIN to select all the rows from the table on the left in the FROM clause (the Customers table). To select all the rows from the table on the right, you use a RIGHT OUTER JOIN as seen in this next example:

```
SELECT Customers.cust_id, Orders.order_num
FROM Customers RIGHT OUTER JOIN Orders
 ON Orders.cust_id = Customers.cust_id;
```

Yet another form of the OUTER JOIN syntax (used by Oracle) requires the use of a + character after the table name as follows:

```
SELECT Customers.cust_id, Orders.order_num
FROM Customers, Orders
WHERE Customers.cust_id  = Orders.cust_id
```

There is one other variant of the outer join, and that is the FULL OUTER JOIN that retrieves all rows from both tables and relates those that can be related. Unlike a LEFT OUTER JOIN or RIGHT OUTER JOIN, which includes unrelated rows from a single table, the FULL OUTER JOIN includes unrelated rows from both tables. The syntax for a FULL OUTER JOIN is as follows:

> **Outer Join Types**   Regardless of the form of outer join used, there are always two basic forms of outer joins—the LEFT OUTER JOIN and the RIGHT OUTER JOIN. The only difference between them is the order of the tables that they are relating. In other words, a LEFT OUTER JOIN can be turned into a RIGHT OUTER JOIN simply by reversing the order of the tables in the FROM or WHERE clause. As such, the two types of outer join can be used interchangeably, and the decision about which one is used is based purely on convenience.

SYNTAX

```
SELECT Customers.cust_id, Orders.order_num
FROM Orders FULL OUTER JOIN Customers
 ON Orders.cust_id = Customers.cust_id;
```

Using Joins with Aggregate Functions

As you learned in Lesson 9, "Summarizing Data," aggregate functions are used to summarize data. Although all the examples of aggregate functions thus far only summarized data from a single table, these functions can also be used with joins.

To demonstrate this, let's look at an example. You want to retrieve a list of all customers and the number of orders that each has placed. The following code uses the COUNT() function to achieve this (Oracle users will have to use a WHERE clause to define the join instead of INNER JOIN):

INPUT

```
SELECT Customers.cust_id, COUNT(Orders.order_num) AS num_ord
FROM Customers INNER JOIN Orders
 ON Customers.cust_id = Orders.cust_id
GROUP BY Customers.cust_id;
```

OUTPUT

```
cust_id          num_ord
---------        --------
1000000001       2
1000000003       1
1000000004       1
1000000005       1
```

ANALYSIS This SELECT statement uses INNER JOIN to relate the customers and orders tables to each other. The GROUP BY clause groups the data by customer, and so the function call COUNT(Orders.order_num) counts the number of orders for each customer and returns it as num_ord.

Aggregate functions can be used just as easily with other join types. See the following example (once again, Oracle users will have to use a WHERE clause to define the join instead of INNER JOIN):

INPUT

```
SELECT Customers.cust_id, COUNT(Orders.order_num) AS num_ord
FROM Customers LEFT OUTER JOIN Orders
 ON Customers.cust_id = Orders.cust_id
GROUP BY Customers.cust_id;
```

OUTPUT

```
cust_id          num_ord
---------        -------
1000000001       2
1000000002       0
1000000003       1
1000000004       1
1000000005       1
```

ANALYSIS This example uses a LEFT OUTER JOIN to include all customers, even those who have not placed any orders. The results show that customer 1000000002 is also included, this time with 0 orders.

Using Joins and Join Conditions

Before I wrap up our two lesson discussion on joins, I think it is worthwhile to summarize some key points regarding joins and their use:

- Pay careful attention to the type of join being used. More often than not, you'll want an inner join, but there are often valid uses for outer joins, too.

- Check your DBMSs documentation for the exact join syntax it supports. (Most DBMSs use one of the forms of syntax described in these two lessons.)

- Make sure you use the correct join condition (regardless of the syntax being used), or you'll return incorrect data.

- Make sure you always provide a join condition, or you'll end up with the Cartesian Product.

- You may include multiple tables in a join and even have different join types for each. Although this is legal and often useful, make sure you test each join separately before testing them together. This will make troubleshooting far simpler.

Summary

This lesson was a continuation of the last lesson on joins. This lesson started by teaching you how and why to use aliases, and then continued with a discussion on different join types and various forms of syntax used with each. You also learned how to use aggregate functions with joins, and some important dos and don'ts to keep in mind when working with joins.

LESSON 14
Combining Queries

In this lesson, you'll learn how to use the UNION operator to combine multiple SELECT statements into one result set.

Understanding Combined Queries

Most SQL queries contain a single SELECT statement that returns data from one or more tables. SQL also enables you to perform multiple queries (multiple SELECT statements) and return the results as a single query result set. These combined queries are usually known as *unions* or *compound queries*.

There are basically two scenarios in which you'd use combined queries:

- To return similarly structured data from different tables in a single query

- To perform multiple queries against a single table returning the data as one query

> **Combining Queries and Multiple WHERE Conditions**
> For the most part, combining two queries to the same table accomplishes the same thing as a single query with multiple WHERE clause conditions. In other words, any SELECT statement with multiple WHERE clauses can also be specified as a combined query, as you'll see in the section that follows.

Creating Combined Queries

SQL queries are combined using the UNION operator. Using UNION, multiple SELECT statements can be specified, and their results can be combined into a single result set.

Using UNION

Using UNION is simple enough. All you do is specify each SELECT statement and place the keyword UNION between each.

Let's look at an example. You need a report on all your customers in Illinois, Indiana, and Michigan. You also want to include all Fun4All locations, regardless of state. Of course, you can create a WHERE clause that will do this, but this time you'll use a UNION instead.

As I just explained, creating a UNION involves writing multiple SELECT statements. First look at the individual statements:

INPUT

```
SELECT cust_name, cust_contact, cust_email
FROM Customers
WHERE cust_state IN ('IL','IN','MI');
```

OUTPUT

```
cust_name           cust_contact        cust_email
----------          -------------       ------------
Village Toys        John Smith          sales@villagetoys.com
Fun4All             Jim Jones           jjones@fun4all.com
The Toy Store       Kim Howard          NULL
```

INPUT

```
SELECT cust_name, cust_contact, cust_email
FROM Customers
WHERE cust_name = 'Fun4All'
```

OUTPUT

```
cust_name           cust_contact        cust_email
-----------         -----------         -------------
Fun4All             Jim Jones           jjones@fun4all.com
Fun4All             Denise L. Stephens  dstephens@fun4all.com
```

ANALYSIS The first SELECT retrieves all rows in Illinois, Indiana, and Michigan by passing those State abbreviations to the IN clause. The second SELECT uses a simple equality test to find all Fun4All locations.

To combine these two statements, do the following:

INPUT

```
SELECT cust_name, cust_contact, cust_email
FROM Customers
WHERE cust_state IN ('IL','IN','MI')
UNION
SELECT cust_name, cust_contact, cust_email
FROM Customers
WHERE cust_name = 'Fun4All';
```

OUTPUT

```
cust_name          cust_contact          cust_email
- - - - - - - - -  - - - - - - - - -     - - - - - - - - - - -
Fun4All            Denise L. Stephens    dstephens@fun4all.com
Fun4All            Jim Jones             jjones@fun4all.com
Village Toys        John Smith            sales@villagetoys.com
The Toy Store      Kim Howard            NULL
```

ANALYSIS The preceding statements is made up of both of the previous SELECT statements separated by the UNION keyword. UNION instructs the DBMS to execute both SELECT statements and combine the output into a single query result set.

As a point of reference, here is the same query using multiple WHERE clauses instead of a UNION:

INPUT

```
SELECT cust_name, cust_contact, cust_email
FROM Customers
WHERE cust_state IN ('IL','IN','MI')
 OR cust_name = 'Fun4All';
```

In our simple example, the UNION might actually be more complicated than using a WHERE clause. But with more complex filtering conditions, or if the data is being retrieved from multiple tables (and not just a single table), the UNION could have made the process much simpler indeed.

UNION Limits There is no standard SQL limit to the number of SELECT statements that can be combined with UNION statements. However, it is best to consult your DBMS documentation to ensure that it does not enforce any maximum statement restrictions of its own.

Performance Issues Most good DBMSs use an internal query optimizer to combine the SELECT statements before they are even processed. In theory, this means that from a performance perspective, there should be no real difference between using multiple WHERE clause conditions or a UNION. I say in theory, because, in practice, most query optimizers don't always do as good a job as they should. Your best bet is to test both methods to see which will work best for you.

UNION Rules

As you can see, unions are very easy to use. But there are a few rules governing exactly which can be combined:

- Each query in a UNION must contain the same columns, expressions, or aggregate functions.

- The columns, expressions, and aggregates must occur in the exact same order in each SELECT statement in a UNION.

- Column datatypes must be compatible: They need not be the exact same type, but they must be of a type that the DBMS can implicitly convert (for example, different numeric types or different date types).

Aside from these basic rules and restrictions, unions can be used for any data retrieval tasks.

Including or Eliminating Duplicate Rows

Go back to the preceding section titled "Using UNION" and look at the sample SELECT statements used. You'll notice that when executed individually, the first SELECT statement returns three rows, and the second SELECT statement returns two rows. However, when the two SELECT statements are combined with a UNION, only four rows are returned, not five.

The UNION automatically removes any duplicate rows from the query result set (in other words, it behaves just as do multiple WHERE clause conditions in a single SELECT would). Because there is a Fun4All location in Indiana, that row was returned by both SELECT statements. When the UNION was used the duplicate row was eliminated.

This is the default behavior of UNION, but you can change this if you so desire. If you would, in fact, want all occurrences of all matches returned, you can use UNION ALL instead of UNION.

Look at the following example:

INPUT

```
SELECT cust_name, cust_contact, cust_email
FROM Customers
WHERE cust_state IN ('IL','IN','MI')
UNION ALL
SELECT cust_name, cust_contact, cust_email
FROM Customers
WHERE cust_name = 'Fun4All';
```

OUTPUT

cust_name	cust_contact	cust_email
Village Toys	John Smith	sales@villagetoys.com
Fun4All	Jim Jones	jjones@fun4all.com
The Toy Store	Kim Howard	NULL
Fun4All	Jim Jones	jjones@fun4all.com
Fun4All	Denise L. Stephens	dstephens@fun4all.com

ANALYSIS Using UNION ALL, the DBMS does not eliminate duplicates. Therefore, the preceding example returns five rows, one of them occurring twice.

> **Tip** At the beginning of this lesson, I said that UNION almost always accomplishes the same thing as multiple WHERE conditions. UNION ALL is the form of UNION that accomplishes what cannot be done with WHERE clauses. If you do, in fact, want all occurrences of matches for every condition (including duplicates), you must use UNION ALL and not WHERE.

Sorting Combined Query Results

SELECT statement output is sorted using the ORDER BY clause. When combining queries with a UNION only one ORDER BY clause may be used, and it must occur after the final SELECT statement. There is very little point in sorting part of a result set one way and part another way, and so multiple ORDER BY clauses are not allowed.

The following example sorts the results returned by the previously used UNION:

INPUT

```
SELECT cust_name, cust_contact, cust_email
FROM Customers
WHERE cust_state IN ('IL','IN','MI')
UNION
SELECT cust_name, cust_contact, cust_email
FROM Customers
WHERE cust_name = 'Fun4All'
ORDER BY cust_name, cust_contact;
```

OUTPUT

```
cust_name        cust_contact        cust_email
-----------      ---------------     -------------
Fun4All          Denise L. Stephens  dstephens@fun4all.com
Fun4All          Jim Jones           jjones@fun4all.com
The Toy Store    Kim Howard          NULL
Village Toys     John Smith          sales@villagetoys.com
```

ANALYSIS This UNION takes a single ORDER BY clause after the final SELECT statement. Even though the ORDER BY appears to only be a part of that last SELECT statement, the DBMS will in fact use it to sort all the results returned by all the SELECT statements.

Summary

In this lesson, you learned how to combine SELECT statements with the UNION operator. Using UNION, you can return the results of multiple queries as one combined query, either including or excluding duplicates. The use of UNION can greatly simplify complex WHERE clauses and retrieving data from multiple tables.

LESSON 15
Inserting Data

In this lesson, you will learn how to insert data into tables using the SQL
INSERT *statement.*

Understanding Data Insertion

SELECT is undoubtedly the most frequently used SQL statement (which is
why the last 14 lessons were dedicated to it). But there are three other
frequently used SQL statements that you should learn. The first one is
INSERT. (You'll get to the other two in the next lesson.)

As its name suggests, INSERT is used to insert (add) rows to a database
table. Insert can be used in several ways:

- Inserting a single complete row

- Inserting a single partial row

- Inserting the results of a query

You'll now look at each of these.

> **INSERT and System Security** Use of the INSERT state-
> ment might require special security privileges in client-
> server DBMSs. Before you attempt to use INSERT, make
> sure you have adequate security privileges to do so.

Inserting Complete Rows

The simplest way to insert data into a table is to use the basic INSERT
syntax, which requires that you specify the table name and the values to
be inserted into the new row. Here is an example of this:

```
INSERT INTO Customers
VALUES('1000000006',
       'Toy Land',
       '123 Any Street',
       'New York',
       'NY',
       '11111',
       NULL,
       NULL);
```

ANALYSIS The above example inserts a new customer into the Customers table. The data to be stored in each table column is specified in the VALUES clause, and a value must be provided for every column. If a column has no value (for example, the cust_contact and cust_email columns above), the NULL value should be used (assuming the table allows no value to be specified for that column). The columns must be populated in the order in which they appear in the table definition.

The INTO Keyword In some SQL implementations, the INTO keyword following INSERT is optional. However, it is good practice to provide this keyword even if it is not needed. Doing so will ensure that your SQL code is portable between DBMSs.

Although this syntax is indeed simple, it is not at all safe and should generally be avoided at all costs. The above SQL statement is highly dependent on the order in which the columns are defined in the table. It also depends on information about that order being readily available. Even if it is available, there is no guarantee that the columns will be in the exact same order the next time the table is reconstructed. Therefore, writing SQL statements that depend on specific column ordering is very unsafe. If you do so, something will inevitably break at some point.

The safer (and unfortunately more cumbersome) way to write the INSERT statement is as follows:

Input

```
INSERT INTO Customers(cust_id,
                      cust_name,
                      cust_address,
                      cust_city,
                      cust_state,
                      cust_zip,
                      cust_contact,
                      cust_email)
VALUES('1000000006',
       'Toy Land',
       '123 Any Street',
       'New York',
       'NY',
       '11111',
       NULL,
       NULL);
```

Analysis This example does the exact same thing as the previous INSERT
statement, but this time the column names are explicitly stated in parentheses after the table name. When the row is inserted the DBMS will
match each item in the columns list with the appropriate value in the
VALUES list. The first entry in VALUES corresponds to the first specified column name. The second value corresponds to the second column name,
and so on.

Because column names are provided, the VALUES must match the specified
column names in the order in which they are specified, and not necessarily in the order that the columns appear in the actual table. The advantage
of this is that, even if the table layout changes, the INSERT statement will
still work correctly.

The following INSERT statement populates all the row columns (just as
before), but it does so in a different order. Because the column names are
specified, the insertion will work correctly:

Input

```
INSERT INTO Customers(cust_id,
                      cust_contact,
                      cust_email,
                      cust_name,
                      cust_address,
                      cust_city,
```

```
                    cust_state,
                    cust_zip)
VALUES('1000000006',
       NULL,
       NULL,
       'Toy Land',
       '123 Any Street',
       'New York',
       'NY',
       '11111');
```

Always Use a Columns List As a rule, never use INSERT without explicitly specifying the column list. This will greatly increase the probability that your SQL will continue to function in the event that table changes occur.

Use VALUES Carefully Regardless of the INSERT syntax being used, the correct number of VALUES must be specified. If no column names are provided, a value must be present for every table column. If columns names are provided, a value must be present for each listed column. If none is present, an error message will be generated, and the row will not be inserted.

Inserting Partial Rows

As I just explained, the recommended way to use INSERT is to explicitly specify table column names. Using this syntax, you can also omit columns. This means you only provide values for some columns, but not for others.

Look at the following example:

INPUT

```
INSERT INTO Customers(cust_id,
                      cust_name,
                      cust_address,
                      cust_city,
                      cust_state,
                      cust_zip)
VALUES('1000000006',
       'Toy Land',
       '123 Any Street',
       'New York',
       'NY',
       '11111');
```

ANALYSIS   In the examples given earlier in this lesson, values were not provided for two of the columns, cust_contact and cust_email. This means there is no reason to include those columns in the INSERT statement. This INSERT statement, therefore, omits the two columns and the two corresponding values.

> **Omitting Columns**   You only omit columns from an INSERT operation if the table definition so allows. One of the following conditions must exist:
>
> * The column is defined as allowing NULL values (no value at all).
>
> * A default value is specified in the table definition. This means the default value will be used if no value is specified.
>
> If you omit a value from a table that does not allow NULL values and does not have a default, the DBMS will generate an error message, and the row will not be inserted.

Inserting Retrieved Data

INSERT is usually used to add a row to a table using specified values. There is another form of INSERT that can be used to insert the result of a SELECT statement into a table. This is known as INSERT SELECT, and, as its name suggests, it is made up of an INSERT statement and a SELECT statement.

Suppose you want to merge a list of customers from another table into your Customers table. Instead of reading one row at a time and inserting it with INSERT, you can do the following:

> **Instructions Needed for the Next Example**   The following example imports data from a table named CustNew into the Customers table. To try this example, create and populate the CustNew table first. The format of the CustNew table should be the same as the Customers table described in Appendix A.

INPUT

```
INSERT INTO Customers(cust_id,
                      cust_contact,
                      cust_email
                      cust_name,
                      cust_address,
                      cust_city,
                      cust_state,
                      cust_zip)
SELECT cust_id,
       cust_contact,
       cust email
       cust_name,
       cust_address,
       cust_city,
       cust_state,
       cust_zip
FROM CustNew;
```

ANALYSIS   This example uses INSERT SELECT to import all the data from CustNew into Customers. Instead of listing the VALUES to be inserted, the SELECT statement retrieves them from CustNew. Each column in the SELECT corresponds to a column in the specified columns list. How many rows will this statement insert? That depends on how many rows are in the CustNew table. If the table is empty, no rows will be inserted (and no error will be generated because the operation is still valid). If the table does, in fact, contain data, all that data is inserted into Customers.

> 💡 **Column Names in INSERT SELECT**   This example uses the same column names in both the INSERT and SELECT statements for simplicity's sake. But there is no requirement that the column names match. In fact, the DBMS does not even pay attention to the column names returned by the SELECT. Rather, the column position is used, so the first column in the SELECT (regardless of its name) will be used to populate the first specified table column, and so on.

The SELECT statement used in an INSERT SELECT can include a WHERE clause to filter the data to be inserted.

> 💡 **Inserting Multiple Rows**   INSERT usually inserts only a single row. To insert multiple rows you must execute multiple INSERT statements. The exception to this rule is INSERT SELECT, which can be used to insert multiple rows with a single statement—whatever the SELECT statement returns will be inserted by the INSERT.

Copying from One Table to Another

There is another form of data insertion that does not use the INSERT statement at all. To copy the contents of a table into a brand new table (one that is created on-the-fly) you can use the SELECT INTO statement.

Unlike INSERT SELECT, which appends data to an existing table, SELECT INTO copies data into a new table (and depending on the DBMS being used, can overwrite the table if it already exists).

The following example demonstrates the use of SELECT INTO:

INPUT

```
SELECT *
INTO CustCopy
FROM Customers;
```

ANALYSIS This SELECT statement creates a new table named CustCopy and copies the entire contents of the Customers table into it. Because SELECT * was used, every column in the Customers table will be created (and populated) in the CustCopy table. To copy only a subset of the available columns, explicit column names can be specified instead of the * wildcard character.

Oracle uses a slightly different syntax:

INPUT

```
CREATE TABLE CustCopy AS
SELECT *
FROM Customers;
```

Here are some things to consider when using SELECT INTO:

- Any SELECT options and clauses may be used including WHERE and GROUP BY.

- Joins may be used to insert data from multiple tables.

- Data may only be inserted into a single table regardless of how many tables the data was retrieved from.

> **Making Copies of Tables** SELECT INTO is a great way to make copies of tables before experimenting with new SQL statements. By making a copy first, you'll be able to test your SQL on that copy instead of on live data.

Summary

In this lesson, you learned how to INSERT rows into a database table. You learned several ways to use INSERT, and why explicit column specification is preferred. You also learned how to use INSERT SELECT to import rows from another table, and how to use SELECT INTO to export rows to a new table. In the next lesson, you'll learn how to use UPDATE and DELETE to further manipulate table data.

LESSON 16

Updating and Deleting Data

In this lesson, you will learn how to use the UPDATE and DELETE statements to enable you to further manipulate your table data.

Updating Data

To update (modify) data in a table the UPDATE statement is used. UPDATE can be used in two ways:

- To update specific rows in a table
- To update all rows in a table

You'll now take a look at each of these uses.

Don't Omit the WHERE Clause Special care must be exercised when using UPDATE, because it is all too easy to mistakenly update every row in your table. Please read this entire section on UPDATE before using this statement.

UPDATE and Security Use of the UPDATE statement might require special security privileges in client-server DBMSs. Before you attempt to use UPDATE, make sure you have adequate security privileges to do so.

The UPDATE statement is very easy to use—some would say too easy. The basic format of an UPDATE statement is made up of three parts:

- The table to be updated

- The column names and their new values

- The filter condition that determines which rows should be updated

Let's take a look at a simple example. Customer 1000000005 now has an email address, and so his record needs updating. The following statement performs this update:

```
UPDATE Customers
SET cust_email = 'kim@thetoystore.com'
WHERE cust_id = '1000000005';
```

ANALYSIS The UPDATE statement always begins with the name of the table being updated. In this example, it is the Customers table. The SET command is then used to assign the new value to a column. As used here, the SET clause sets the cust_email column to the specified value:

```
SET cust_email = 'kim@thetoystore.com'
```

The UPDATE statement finishes with a WHERE clause that tells the DBMS which row to update. Without a WHERE clause, the DBMS would update all the rows in the Customers table with this new email address—definitely not the desired effect.

Updating multiple columns requires a slightly different syntax:

```
UPDATE Customers
SET cust_contact = 'Sam Roberts',
    cust_email = 'sam@toyland.com'
WHERE cust_id = '1000000006';
```

ANALYSIS When updating multiple columns, only a single SET command is used, and each column = value pair is separated by a comma. (No comma is specified after the last column.) In this example, columns cust_contact and cust_email will both be updated for customer 1000000006.

Using Subqueries in an UPDATE Statement   Subqueries may be used in UPDATE statements, enabling you to update columns with data retrieved with a SELECT statement. Refer back to Lesson 11, "Working with Subqueries," for more information on subqueries and their uses.

The FROM Keyword   Some SQL implementations support a FROM clause in the UPDATE statement that can be used to update the rows in one table with data from another table. Refer to your DBMS documentation to see if it supports this feature.

To delete a column's value, you can set it to NULL (assuming the table is defined to allow NULL values). You can do this as follows:

INPUT

```
UPDATE Customers
SET cust_email = NULL
WHERE cust_id = '1000000005';
```

ANALYSIS   Here the NULL keyword is used to save no value to the cust_email column.

Deleting Data

To delete (remove) data from a table, the DELETE statement is used. DELETE can be used in two ways:

- To delete specific rows from a table

- To delete all rows from a table

You'll now take a look at each of these.

Don't Omit the WHERE Clause   Special care must be exercised when using DELETE because it is all too easy to mistakenly delete every row from your table. Please read this entire section on DELETE before using this statement.

DELETE and Security   Use of the DELETE statement might require special security privileges in client-server DBMSs. Before you attempt to use DELETE, make sure you have adequate security privileges to do so.

I already stated that UPDATE is very easy to use. The good (and bad) news is that DELETE is even easier to use.

The following statement deletes a single row from the Customers table:

INPUT

```
DELETE FROM Customers
WHERE cust_id = '1000000006';
```

ANALYSIS   This statement should be self-explanatory. DELETE FROM requires that you specify the name of the table from which the data is to be deleted. The WHERE clause filters which rows are to be deleted. In this example, only customer 1000000006 will be deleted. If the WHERE clause were omitted, this statement would have deleted every customer in the table.

The FROM Keyword   In some SQL implementations, the FROM keyword following DELETE is optional. However, it is good practice to always provide this keyword, even if it is not needed. Doing this will ensure that your SQL code is portable between DBMSs.

DELETE takes no column names or wildcard characters. DELETE deletes entire rows, not columns. To delete specific columns use an UPDATE statement.

Guidelines for Updating and Deleting Data

The UPDATE and DELETE statements used in the previous section all have WHERE clauses, and there is a very good reason for this. If you omit the WHERE clause, the UPDATE or DELETE will be applied to every row in the table. In other words, if you execute an UPDATE without a WHERE clause, every row in the table will be updated with the new values. Similarly if you execute DELETE without a WHERE clause, all the contents of the table will be deleted.

Here are some important guidelines that many SQL programmers follow:

- Never execute an UPDATE or a DELETE without a WHERE clause unless you really do intend to update and delete every row.

- Make sure every table has a primary key (refer back to Lesson 12, "Joining Tables," if you have forgotten what this is), and use it as the WHERE clause whenever possible. (You may specify individual primary keys, multiple values, or value ranges.)

- Before you use a WHERE clause with an UPDATE or a DELETE, first test it with a SELECT to make sure it is filtering the right records—it is far too easy to write incorrect WHERE clauses.

- Use database enforced referential integrity (refer back to Lesson 12 for this one, too) so that the DBMS will not allow the deletion of rows that have data in other tables related to them.

- Some DBMSs allow database administrators to impose restrictions that prevent the execution of UPDATE or DELETE without a WHERE clause. If your DBMS supports this feature, consider using it.

The bottom line is that SQL has no Undo button. Be very careful using UPDATE and DELETE, or you'll find yourself updating and deleting the wrong data.

Summary

In this lesson, you learned how to use the UPDATE and DELETE statements to manipulate the data in your tables. You learned the syntax for each of these statements, as well as the inherent dangers they expose. You also learned why WHERE clauses are so important in UPDATE and DELETE statements, and you were given guidelines that should be followed to help ensure that data does not get damaged inadvertently.

LESSON 17

Creating and Manipulating Tables

In this lesson you'll learn the basics of table creation, alteration, and deletion.

Creating Tables

SQL is not just used for table data manipulation. Rather, SQL can be used to perform all database and table operations, including the creation and manipulation of tables themselves.

There are generally two ways to create database tables:

- Most DBMSs come with an administration tool that can be used to create and manage database tables interactively.

- Tables may also be manipulated directly with SQL statements.

To create tables programmatically, the CREATE TABLE SQL statement is used. It is worth noting that when you use interactive tools, you are actually using SQL statements. Instead of your writing these statements, however, the interface generates and executes the SQL seamlessly for you (the same is true for changes to existing tables).

> **Syntax Differences**   The exact syntax of the CREATE TABLE statement can vary from one SQL implementation to another. Be sure to refer to your DBMS documentation for more information on exactly what syntax and features it supports.

Complete coverage of all the options available when creating tables is beyond the scope of this lesson, but here are the basics. I'd recommend that you review your DBMS documentation for more information and specifics.

Basic Table Creation

To create a table using CREATE TABLE, you must specify the following information:

- The name of the new table specified after the keywords CREATE TABLE

- The name and definition of the table columns separated by commas

- Some DBMSs require that you also specify the table location

The following SQL statement creates the Products table used throughout this book:

`INPUT`

```
CREATE TABLE Products
(
    prod_id         CHAR(10)       NOT NULL,
    vend_id         CHAR(10)       NOT NULL,
    prod_name     CHAR(255)     NOT NULL,
    prod_price     DECIMAL(8,2)     NOT NULL,
    prod_desc     VARCHAR
);
```

`ANALYSIS` As you can see in the above statement, the table name is specified immediately preceding the CREATE TABLE keywords. The actual table definition (all the columns) is enclosed within parentheses. The columns themselves are separated by commas. This particular table is made up of five columns. Each column definition starts with the column name (which must be unique within the table), followed by the column's datatype. (Refer to Lesson 1, "Understanding SQL," for an explanation of datatypes. In addition, Appendix D, "Using SQL Datatypes," lists commonly used datatypes and their compatibility.) The entire statement is terminated with a semicolon after the closing parenthesis.

> **Statement Formatting**   As you will recall, whitespace is ignored in SQL statements. Statements can be typed on one long line or broken up over many lines. It makes no difference at all. This enables you to format your SQL as best suits you. The preceding CREATE TABLE statement is a good example of SQL statement formatting—the code is specified over multiple lines, with the column definitions indented for easier reading and editing. Formatting your SQL in this way is entirely optional, but highly recommended.

> **Replacing Existing Tables**   When you create a new table, the table name specified must not exist or you'll generate an error. To prevent accidental overwriting, SQL requires that you first manually remove a table (see later sections for details) and then recreate it, rather than just overwriting it.

Working with NULL Values

Back in Lesson 4, "Filtering Data," you learned that NULL values are no values or the lack of a value. A column that allows NULL values also allows rows to be inserted with no value at all in that column. A column that does not allow NULL values does not accept rows with no value—in other words, that column will always be required when rows are inserted or updated.

Every table column is either a NULL column or a NOT NULL column, and that state is specified in the table definition at creation time. Take a look at the following example:

INPUT

```
CREATE TABLE Orders
(
    order_num      INTEGER        NOT NULL,
    order_date     DATETIME       NOT NULL,
    cust_id        CHAR(10)       NOT NULL
);
```

ANALYSIS This statement creates the Orders table used throughout this book. Orders contains three columns: order number, order date, and the customer ID. All three columns are required, and so each contains the keyword NOT NULL. This will prevent the insertion of columns with no value. If someone tries to insert no value, an error will be returned, and the insertion will fail.

This next example creates a table with a mixture of NULL and NOT NULL columns:

INPUT

```
CREATE TABLE Vendors
(
    vend_id          CHAR(10)      NOT NULL,
    vend_name      CHAR(50)      NOT NULL,
    vend_address     CHAR(50)        ,
    vend_city      CHAR(50)      ,
    vend_state     CHAR          ,
    vend_zip       CHAR(10)
);
```

ANALYSIS This statement creates the Vendors table used throughout this book. The vendor ID and vendor name columns are both required, and are, therefore, specified as NOT NULL. The four remaining columns all allow NULL values, and so NOT NULL is not specified. NULL is the default setting, so if NOT NULL is not specified NULL is assumed.

Specifying NULL Most DBMSs treat the absence of NOT NULL to mean NULL. However, not all do. Some require the keyword NULL and will generate an error if it is not specified. Refer to your DBMS documentation for complete syntax information.

Primary Keys and NULL Values Back in Lesson 1, "Understanding SQL," you learned that primary keys are columns whose values uniquely identify every row in a table. Only columns that do not allow NULL values can be used in primary keys. Columns that allow no value at all cannot be used as unique identifiers.

> **Understanding NULL**   Don't confuse NULL values
> with empty strings. A NULL value is the lack of a value;
> it is not an empty string. If you were to specify ' '
> (two single quotes with nothing in between them),
> that would be allowed in a NOT NULL column. An
> empty string is a valid value; it is not no value. NULL
> values are specified with the keyword NULL, not with
> an empty string.

Specifying Default Values

SQL enables you to specify default values to be used if no value is specified when a row is inserted. Default values are specified using the
DEFAULT keyword in the column definitions in the CREATE TABLE
statement.

Look at the following example:

`INPUT`

```
CREATE TABLE OrderItems
(
    order_num    INTEGER        NOT NULL,
    order_item   INTEGER         NOT NULL,
    prod_id       CHAR(10)     NOT NULL,
    quantity     INTEGER        NOT NULL    DEFAULT 1,
    item_price    DECIMAL(8,2)    NOT NULL
);
```

`ANALYSIS`   This statement creates the OrderItems table that contains the
individual items that make up an order. (The order itself is stored in the
Orders table.) The quantity column contains the quantity for each item
in an order. In this example, adding the text DEFAULT 1 to the column
description instructs the DBMS to use a quantity of 1 if no quantity is
specified.

Default values are often used to store values in date or time stamp
columns. Look at the following example:

```
CREATE TABLE Orders
(
    order_num     INTEGER          NOT NULL,
    order_date    DATE             NOT NULL     DEFAULT sysdate,
    cust_id       CHAR(10)         NOT NULL
);
```

ANALYSIS This is an Oracle statement that creates the same Orders table
as above. (You'll notice that the datatype for the order_date field is DATE
instead of DATETIME. See Appendix D for more information.) The big difference here is that a default order date is specified. Default values may
be any valid expression—literal strings, variables, or functions. Here the
Oracle global variable sysdate is used. (In Oracle, sysdate always
returns the current system date and time, so if no order date is specified
the current date is used.)

Here is the same example in SQL Server:

```
CREATE TABLE Orders
(
    order_num     INTEGER          NOT NULL,
    order_date    DATETIME         NOT NULL     DEFAULT GETDATE(),
    cust_id       CHAR(10)         NOT NULL
);
```

ANALYSIS SQL Server does not have a sysdate variable, but it does have
a function called GETDATE() that returns the current system date and time.
By specifying DEFAULT GETDATE(), you tell the DBMS to execute the
GETDATE() function and use the returned value.

Using DEFAULT Instead of NULL Values   Many database
developers use DEFAULT values instead of NULL columns,
especially in columns that will be used in
calculations or data groupings.

Updating Tables

To update table definitions, the ALTER TABLE statement is used. Although all DBMSs support ALTER TABLE, what they allow you to alter varies dramatically from one to another. Here are some points to consider when using ALTER TABLE:

- Tables should never be altered after they contain data. You should spend sufficient time anticipating future needs during the table design process so that extensive changes are not required later on.

- All DBMSs allow you to add columns to existing tables, although some restrict the datatypes that may be added (as well as NULL and DEFAULT usage).

- Many DBMSs do not allow you to remove or change columns in a table.

- Most DBMSs allow you to rename columns.

- Many DBMSs restrict the kinds of changes you can make on columns that are populated and enforce fewer restrictions on unpopulated columns.

As you can see, making changes to existing tables is neither simple nor consistent. Be sure to refer to your own DBMS documentation to determine exactly what you can alter.

To change a table using ALTER TABLE, you must specify the following information:

- The name of the table to be altered after the keywords ALTER TABLE. (The table must exist or an error will be generated.)

- The list of changes to be made.

Because adding columns to an existing table is about the only operation supported by all DBMSs, I'll use that for an example:

INPUT

```
ALTER TABLE Vendors
ADD vend_phone CHAR(20);
```

ANALYSIS This statement adds a column named vend_phone to the Vendors table. The datatype must be specified.

Other alter operations, for example, changing or dropping columns, or adding constraints or keys, use a similar syntax. (Note that the following example will not work with all DBMSs):

INPUT

```
ALTER TABLE Vendors
DROP COLUMN vend_phone;
```

Complex table structure changes usually requires a manual move process involving these steps:

- Create a new table with the new column layout.

- Use the INSERT SELECT statement (see Lesson 15, "Inserting Data," for details of this statement) to copy the data from the old table to the new table. Use conversion functions and calculated fields, if needed.

- Verify that the new table contains the desired data.

- Rename the old table (or delete it, if you are really brave).

- Rename the new table with the name previously used by the old table.

- Recreate any triggers, stored procedures, indexes, and foreign keys as needed.

Use ALTER TABLE Carefully Use ALTER TABLE with extreme caution, and be sure you have a complete set of backups (both schema and data) before proceeding. Database table changes cannot be undone—and if you add columns you don't need, you might not be able to remove them. Similarly, if you drop a column that you do need, you might lose all the data in that column.

Deleting Tables

Deleting tables (actually removing the entire table, not just the contents) is very easy—arguably too easy. Tables are deleted using the DROP TABLE statement:

INPUT

```
DROP TABLE CustCopy;
```

ANALYSIS This statement deletes the CustCopy table. (You created that one in Lesson 15.) There is no confirmation, nor is there an undo—executing the statement will permanently remove the table.

> **Using Relational Rules to Prevent Accidental Deletion**
> Many DBMSs allow you to enforce rules that prevent the dropping of tables that are related to other tables. When these rules are enforced, if you issue a DROP TABLE statement against a table that is part of a relationship, the DBMS blocks the operation until the relationship was removed. It is a good idea to enable these options, if available, to prevent the accidental dropping of needed tables.

Renaming Tables

Table renaming is supported differently by each DBMS. There is no hard and fast standard for this operation. Oracle users can use the RENAME statement, SQL Server users can use the supplied sp_rename stored procedure. Refer to your own DBMS documentation for details on supported syntax.

Summary

In this lesson, you learned several new SQL statements. CREATE TABLE is used to create new tables, ALTER TABLE is used to change table columns (or other objects like constraints or indexes), and DROP TABLE is used to completely delete a table. These statements should be used with extreme caution, and only after backups have been made. As the exact syntax of each of these statements varies from one DBMS to another, you should consult your own DBMS documentation for more information.

LESSON 18
Using Views

In this lesson you'll learn exactly what views are, how they work, and when they should be used. You'll also see how views can be used to simplify some of the SQL operations performed in earlier lessons.

Understanding Views

Views are virtual tables. Unlike tables that contain data, views simply contain queries that dynamically retrieve data when used.

The best way to understand views is to look at an example. Back in Lesson 12, "Joining Tables," you used the following SELECT statement to retrieve data from three tables:

INPUT
```
SELECT cust_name, cust_contact
FROM Customers, Orders, OrderItems
WHERE Customers.cust_id = Orders.cust_id
 AND OrderItems.order_num = Orders.order_num
 AND prod_id = 'RGAN01';
```

That query was used to retrieve the customers who had ordered a specific product. Anyone needing this data would have to understand the table structure, as well as how to create the query and join the tables. To retrieve the same data for another product (or for multiple products), the last WHERE clause would have to be modified.

Now imagine that you could wrap that entire query in a virtual table called ProductCustomers. You could then simply do the following to retrieve the same data:

INPUT
```
SELECT cust_name, cust_contact
FROM ProductCustomers
WHERE prod_id = 'RGAN01';
```

This is where views come into play. ProductCustomers is a view, and as a view, it does not contain any columns or data. Instead it contains a query—the same query used above to join the tables properly.

 DBMS Consistency   You'll be relieved to know that view creation syntax is supported pretty consistently by all the major DBMSs.

Why Use Views

You've already seen one use for views. Here are some other common uses:

- To reuse SQL statements.

- To simplify complex SQL operations. After the query is written, it can be reused easily, without having to know the details of the underlying query itself.

- To expose parts of a table instead of complete tables.

- To secure data. Users can be given access to specific subsets of tables instead of to entire tables.

- To change data formatting and representation. Views can return data formatted differently from their underlying tables.

For the most part, after views are created, they can be used in the same way as tables. You can perform SELECT operations, filter and sort data, join views to other views or tables, and possibly even add and update data. (There are some restrictions on this last item. More on that in a moment.)

The important thing to remember is views are just that, views into data stored elsewhere. Views contain no data themselves, so the data they return is retrieved from other tables. When data is added or changed in those tables, the views will return that changed data.

> **Performance Issues**   Because views contain no data, any retrieval needed to execute a query must be processed every time the view is used. If you create complex views with multiple joins and filters, or if you nest views, you may find that performance is dramatically degraded. Be sure you test execution before deploying applications that use views extensively.

View Rules and Restrictions

Before you create views yourself, there are some restrictions of which you should be aware. Unfortunately, the restrictions tend to be very DBMS specific, so check your own DBMS documentation before proceeding.

Here are some of the most common rules and restrictions governing view creation and usage:

- Like tables, views must be uniquely named. (They cannot be named with the name of any other table or view.)

- There is no limit to the number of views that can be created.

- To create views, you must have security access. This is usually granted by the database administrator.

- Views can be nested; that is, a view may be built using a query that retrieves data from another view. The exact number of nested levels allowed varies from DBMS to DBMS. (Some DBMS nesting views can seriously degrade query performance, so test this thoroughly before using it in production environments.)

- Many DBMSs prohibit the use of the ORDER BY clause in view queries.

- Some DBMSs require that every column returned be named— this will require the use of aliases if columns are calculated fields. (See Lesson 7, "Creating Calculated Fields," for more information on column aliases.)

- Views cannot be indexed, nor can they have triggers or default values associated with them.

- Some DBMSs treat views as read-only queries—meaning you can retrieve data from views but not write data back to the underlying tables. Refer to your DBMS documentation for details.

- Some DBMSs allow you to create views that do not allow rows to be inserted or updated if that insertion or update will cause that row to no longer be part of the view. For example, if you have a view that retrieves only customers with email addresses, updating a customer to remove his email address would make that customer fall out of the view. This is the default behavior and is allowed, but depending on your DBMS you might be able to prevent this from occurring.

> **Refer to Your DBMS Documentation** That's a long list of rules, and your own DBMS documentation will likely contain additional rules, too. It is worth taking the time to understand what restrictions you must adhere to before creating views.

Creating Views

So now that you know what views are (and the rules and restrictions that govern them), let's look at view creation.

Views are created using the CREATE VIEW statement. Like CREATE TABLE, CREATE VIEW can only be used to create a view that does not exist. To overwrite a view you must first DROP it and then recreate it.

Using Views to Simplify Complex Joins

One of the most common uses of views is to hide complex SQL, and this often involves joins. Look at the following statement:

```
CREATE VIEW ProductCustomers AS
SELECT cust_name, cust_contact, prod_id
FROM Customers, Orders, OrderItems
WHERE Customers.cust_id = Orders.cust_id
 AND OrderItems.order_num = Orders.order_num;
```

ANALYSIS   This statement creates a view named `ProductCustomers`, which joins three tables to return a list of all customers who have ordered any product. If you were to `SELECT * FROM ProductCustomers`, you'd list every customer who ordered anything.

CREATE VIEW and Semicolons   Unlike most SQL statements, Microsoft SQL Server does not support the use of a semicolon after a `CREATE VIEW` statement.

To retrieve a list of customers who ordered product `RGAN01` you can do the following:

```
SELECT cust_name, cust_contact
FROM ProductCustomers
WHERE prod_id = 'RGAN01';
```

```
cust_name                 cust_contact
------------------        ------------------
Fun4All                   Denise L. Stephens
The Toy Store             Kim Howard
```

ANALYSIS   This statement retrieves specific data from the view by issuing a `WHERE` clause. When the DBMS processes the request, it adds the specified `WHERE` clause to any existing `WHERE` clauses in the view query so that the data is filtered correctly.

As you can see, views can greatly simplify the use of complex SQL statements. Using views, you can write the underlying SQL once and then reuse it as needed.

> **Creating Reusable Views**   It is a good idea to create
> views that are not tied to specific data. For example,
> the view created above returns customers for all prod-
> ucts, not just product RGAN01 (for which the view was
> first created). Expanding the scope of the view
> enables it to be reused, making it even more useful. It
> also eliminates the need for you to create and main-
> tain multiple similar views.

Using Views to Reformat Retrieved Data

As mentioned above, another common use of views is for reformatting
retrieved data. The following SELECT statement returns mailing address
information for all customers in the Customers table:

INPUT

```
SELECT  cust_name,      cust_address,
        cust_city,
        cust_state,
        cust_zip
FROM Customers
```

OUTPUT

cust_name	cust_address	cust_city	cust_state	cust_zip
Village Toys	200 Maple Lane	Detroit	MI	44444
Kids Place	333 South Lake Dr	Columbus	OH	43333
Fun4All	1 Sunny Place	Muncie	IN	42222
Fun4All	829 Riverside Dr	Phoenix	AZ	88888
The Toy Store	4545 53rd Street	Chicago	IL	54545
Toys Emporium	NULL	NULL	NULL	NULL

Suppose you must print labels regularly using this data. The mailing
labels need three lines: one for the name and one for each line of the
address. The second address line must be formatted correctly (comma
and space between city and state, and space between state and zip). The
following SQL statement could be used to return the three lines formatted
as needed:

```
SELECT cust_name,
       cust_address AS cust_address1,
       RTRIM(cust_city) + ', ' + RTRIM(cust_state) + ' ' +
       ➥RTRIM(cust_zip) AS cust_address2
       FROM Customers
```

cust_name	cust_address1	cust_address2
Village Toys	200 Maple Lane	Detroit, MI 44444
Kids Place	333 South Lake Drive	Columbus, OH 43333
Fun4All	1 Sunny Place	Muncie, IN 42222
Fun4All	829 Riverside Drive	Phoenix, AZ 88888
The Toy Store	4545 53rd Street	Chicago, IL 54545
Toys Emporium	NULL	NULL

This statement returns three columns: cust_name is returned as is, cust_address1 is cust_address renamed with an alias for consistency, and cust_address3 is calculated using three other columns.

To turn this into a view, you can do the following:

```
CREATE VIEW CustomerMailingLables AS
SELECT   cust_name,
         cust_address AS cust_address1,
         RTRIM(cust_city) + ', ' + RTRIM(cust_state)
         + ' ' + RTRIM(cust_zip) AS cust_address2
FROM Customers;
```

Here's the Oracle version of this statement:

```
CREATE VIEW CustomerMailingLables AS
SELECT   cust_name,
         cust_address AS cust_address1,
         RTRIM(cust_city) || ', ' || RTRIM(cust_state)
         || ' ' || RTRIM(cust_zip) AS cust_address2
FROM Customers;
```

ANALYSIS This statement creates a view using the exact same query as the previous SELECT statement. To retrieve the data to create all mailing labels, simply do the following:

INPUT

```
SELECT *
FROM CustomerMailingLables;
```

OUTPUT

```
cust_name          cust_address1          cust_address2
------------       --------------------   ------------------
Village Toys       200 Maple Lane         Detroit, MI 44444
Kids Place         333 South Lake Drive   Columbus, OH 43333
Fun4All            1 Sunny Place          Muncie, IN 42222
Fun4All            829 Riverside Drive    Phoenix, AZ 88888
The Toy Store      4545 53rd Street       Chicago, IL 54545
Toys Emporium      NULL                   NULL
```

You'll notice in the above output that one of the addresses is incomplete (the row that we added in Lesson 16, "Updating and Deleting Data"). You might want to define the CustomerMailingLabels view so that it filters out any incomplete addresses. (They cannot be used for mailing labels anyway.) To do this, you can use the following statement (you'll have to first DROP the view to remove it as explained above):

INPUT

```
CREATE VIEW CustomerMailingLables AS
SELECT  cust_name,
        cust_address AS cust_address1,
        RTRIM(cust_city) + ', ' + RTRIM(cust_state)
          + ' ' + RTRIM(cust_zip) AS cust_address2
FROM Customers
WHERE NOT cust_address IS NULL
 AND NOT cust_city IS NULL
 AND NOT cust_state IS NULL
 AND NOT cust_zip IS NULL;
```

OUTPUT

```
cust_name          cust_address1          cust_address2
------------       --------------------   ------------------
Village Toys       200 Maple Lane         Detroit, MI 44444
Kids Place         333 South Lake Drive   Columbus, OH 43333
Fun4All            1 Sunny Place          Muncie, IN 42222
Fun4All            829 Riverside Drive    Phoenix, AZ 88888
The Toy Store      4545 53rd Street       Chicago, IL 54545
```

Using Views with Calculated Fields

Views are exceptionally useful for simplifying the use of calculated fields. The following is a SELECT statement introduced in Lesson 7, "Creating Calculated Fields." It retrieves the order items for a specific order, calculating the expanded price for each item:

INPUT

```
SELECT  prod_id,
        quantity,
        item_price,
        quantity*item_price AS expanded_price
FROM OrderItems
WHERE order_num = 20008;
```

OUTPUT

```
prod_id        quantity       item_price       expanded_price
----------     -----------    ----------------------------------------
RGAN01         5              4.9900           24.9500
BR03           5              11.9900          59.9500
BNBG01         10             3.4900           34.9000
BNBG02         10             3.4900           34.9000
BNBG03         10             3.4900           34.9000
```

To turn this into a view, do the following:

INPUT

```
CREATE VIEW OrderItemsExpanded AS
SELECT  order_num,
        prod_id,
        quantity,
        item_price,
        quantity*item_price AS expanded_price
FROM OrderItems;
```

To retrieve the details for order 20008 (the output above), do the following:

INPUT

```
SELECT *
FROM OrderItemsExpanded
WHERE order_num = 20008;
```

OUTPUT				
order_num	prod_id	quantity	item_price	expanded_price
20008	RGAN01	5	4.99	24.95
20008	BR03	5	11.99	59.95
20008	BNBG01	10	3.49	34.90
20008	BNBG02	10	3.49	34.90
20008	BNBG03	10	3.49	34.90

As you can see, views are easy to create and even easier to use. Used correctly, views can greatly simplify complex data manipulation.

Summary

Views are virtual tables. They do not contain data, but instead, they contain queries that retrieve data as needed. Views provide a level of encapsulation around SQL SELECT statements and can be used to simplify data manipulation, as well as to reformat or secure underlying data.

LESSON 19

Using Transaction Processing

In this lesson, you'll learn what transactions are and how to use COMMIT *and* ROLLBACK *statements to manage transaction processing.*

Understanding Transaction Processing

Transaction processing is used to maintain database integrity by ensuring that batches of SQL operations execute completely or not at all.

As explained back in Lesson 12, "Joining Tables," relational databases are designed so that data is stored in multiple tables to facilitate easier data manipulation, management, and reuse. Without going in to the hows and whys of relational database design, take it as a given that well-designed database schemas are relational to some degree.

The Orders tables that you've been using in the past 18 lessons are a good example of this. Orders are stored in two tables: Orders stores actual orders, and OrderItems stores the individual items ordered. These two tables are related to each other using unique IDs called primary keys (as discussed in Lesson 1, "Understanding SQL"). These tables, in turn, are related to other tables containing customer and product information.

The process of adding an order to the system is as follows:

1. Check if the customer is already in the database. If not, add him.

2. Retrieve the customer's ID.

3. Add a row to the Orders table associating it with the customer ID.

4. Retrieve the new order ID assigned in the Orders table.

5. Add one row to the OrderItems table for each item ordered, associating it with the Orders table by the retrieved ID (and with the Products table by product ID).

Now imagine that some database failure (for example, out of disk space, security restrictions, table locks) prevents this entire sequence from completing. What would happen to your data?

Well, if the failure occurred after the customer was added and before the Orders table was added, there is no real problem. It is perfectly valid to have customers without orders. When you run the sequence again, the inserted customer record will be retrieved and used. You can effectively pick up where you left off.

But what if the failure occurred after the Orders row was added, but before the OrderItems rows were added? Now you'd have an empty order sitting in your database.

Worse, what if the system failed during adding the OrderItems rows? Now you'd end up with a partial order in your database, but you wouldn't know it.

How do you solve this problem? That's where Transaction Processing comes in. Transaction Processing is a mechanism used to manage sets of SQL operations that must be executed in batches so as to ensure that databases never contain the results of partial operations. With Transaction Processing, you can ensure that sets of operations are not aborted midprocessing—they either execute in their entirety or not at all. If no error occurs, the entire set of statements is committed (written) to the database tables. If an error does occur, then a rollback (undo) can occur to restore the database to a known and safe state.

So, looking at the same example, this is how the process would work:

1. Check if the customer is already in the database; if not add him.

2. Commit the customer information.

3. Retrieve the customer's ID.

4. Add a row to the Orders table.

5. If a failure occurs while adding the row to Orders, roll back.

6. Retrieve the new order ID assigned in the Orders table.

7. Add one row to the OrderItems table for each item ordered.

8. If a failure occurs while adding rows to OrderItems, roll back all the OrderItems rows added and the Orders row.

When working with transactions and transaction processing, there are a few keywords that'll keep reappearing. Here are the terms you need to know:

- *Transaction*   A block of SQL statements

- *Rollback*   The process of undoing passed SQL statements

- *Commit*   Writing unsaved SQL statements to the database tables

- *Savepoint*   A temporary placeholder in a transaction set to which you can issue a rollback (as opposed to rolling back an entire transaction)

> **Which Statements Can You Roll Back?**   Transaction processing is used to manage INSERT, UPDATE, and DELETE statements. You cannot roll back SELECT statements. (There would not be much point in doing so anyway.) You cannot roll back CREATE or DROP operations. These statements may be used in a transaction block, but if you perform a rollback they will not be undone.

Controlling Transactions

Now that you know what transactions processing is, let's look at what is involved in managing transactions.

Implementation Differences   The exact syntax used to implement transaction processing differs from one DBMS to another. Refer to your DBMS documentation before proceeding.

The key to managing transactions involves breaking your SQL statements into logical chunks and explicitly stating when data should be rolled back and when it should not.

Some DBMSs require that you explicitly mark the start and end of transaction blocks. In SQL Server, for example, you can do the following:

INPUT

```
BEGIN TRANSACTION
...
COMMIT TRANSACTION
```

In this example, any SQL between the BEGIN TRANSACTION and COMMIT TRANSACTION statements must be executed entirely or not at all.

Using ROLLBACK

The SQL ROLLBACK command is used to roll back (undo) SQL statements, as seen in this next statement:

INPUT

```
DELETE FROM Orders;
ROLLBACK;
```

In this example, a DELETE operation is performed and then undone using a ROLLBACK statement. Although not the most useful example, it does demonstrate that, within a transaction block, DELETE operations (like INSERT and UPDATE operations) are never final.

Using COMMIT

Usually SQL statements are executed and written directly to the database tables. This is known as an *implicit commit*—the commit (write or save) operation happens automatically.

Within a transaction block, however, commits might not occur implicitly. This, too, is DBMS specific. Some DBMSs treat a transaction end as an implicit commit; others do not.

To force an explicit commit, the COMMIT statement is used. The following is a SQL Server example:

INPUT

```
BEGIN TRANSACTION
DELETE OrderItems WHERE order_num = 12345
DELETE Orders WHERE order_num = 12345
COMMIT TRANSACTION
```

ANALYSIS   In this SQL Server example, order number 12345 is deleted entirely from the system. Because this involves updating two database tables, Orders and OrderItems, a transaction block is used to ensure that the order is not partially deleted. The final COMMIT statement writes the change only if no error occurred. If the first DELETE worked, but the second failed, the DELETE would not be committed.

To accomplish the same thing in Oracle, you can do the following:

INPUT

```
DELETE OrderItems WHERE order_num = 12345;
DELETE Orders WHERE order_num = 12345;
COMMIT;
```

Using Savepoints

Simple ROLLBACK and COMMIT statements enable you to write or undo an entire transaction. Although this works for simple transactions, more complex transactions might require partial commits or rollbacks.

For example, the process of adding an order described previously is a single transaction. If an error occurs, you only want to roll back to the point before the Orders row was added. You do not want to roll back the addition to the Customers table (if there was one).

To support the rollback of partial transactions, you must be able to put placeholders at strategic locations in the transaction block. Then, if a rollback is required, you can roll back to one of the placeholders.

In SQL, these placeholders are called savepoints. To create one in Oracle, the SAVEPOINT statement is used, as follows:

INPUT

```
SAVEPOINT delete1;
```

In SQL Server, you do the following:

INPUT

```
SAVE TRANSACTION delete1;
```

Each savepoint takes a unique name that identifies it so that, when you roll back, the DBMS knows where you are rolling back to. To roll back to this savepoint, do the following in SQL Server:

INPUT

```
ROLLBACK TRANSACTION delete1;
```

In Oracle you can do the following:

INPUT

```
ROLLBACK TO delete1;
```

The following is a complete SQL Server example:

INPUT

```
BEGIN TRANSACTION
INSERT INTO Customers(cust_id,cust_name)
VALUES('1000000010','Toys Emporium');
SAVE TRANSACTION StartOrder;
INSERT INTO Orders(order_num,order_date,cust_id)
VALUES(20100,'1999/12/1','1000000010');
IF @@ERROR <> 0 ROLLBACK TRANSACTION StartOrder;
INSERT INTO
OrderItems(order_num,order_item,prod_id,quantity,item_price)
VALUES(20010,1,'BR01',100,5.49);
IF @@ERROR <> 0 ROLLBACK TRANSACTION StartOrder;
INSERT INTO
OrderItems(order_num,order_item,prod_id,quantity,item_price)
VALUES(20010,2,'BR03',100,10.99);
IF @@ERROR <> 0 ROLLBACK TRANSACTION StartOrder;
COMMIT TRANSACTION
```

ANALYSIS   Here are a set of four INSERT statements enclosed within a transaction block. A savepoint is defined after the first INSERT so that, if any of the subsequent INSERT operations fail, the transaction is only rolled back that far. In SQL Server, a variable named @@ERROR can be inspected to see if an operation succeeded. (Other DBMSs use different functions or variables to return this information.) If @@ERROR returns a value other than 0, an error occurred, and the transaction rolls back to the savepoint. If the entire transaction is processed, a COMMIT is issued to save the data.

Summary

In this lesson, you learned that transactions are blocks of SQL statements that must be executed as a batch. You learned how to use the COMMIT and ROLLBACK statements to explicitly manage when data is written and when it is undone. You also learned how to use savepoints to provide a greater level of control over rollback operations.

LESSON 20

Understanding Advanced SQL Features

In this lesson, you'll look at several of the advanced data manipulation features that have evolved with SQL—constraints, indexes, stored procedures, and triggers.

Understanding Constraints

SQL has evolved through many versions to become a very complete and powerful language. Many of these more powerful features are sophisticated database manipulation tools that provide you with data manipulation techniques such as constraints.

Relational tables and referential integrity have both been discussed several times in prior lessons. As I explained in those lessons, relational databases store data broken into multiple tables, each of which stores related data. Keys are used to create references from one table to the other (and thus the term referential integrity).

For relational database designs to work properly, you need a way to ensure that only valid data is inserted into tables. For example, if the Orders table stores order information, and OrderItems stores order details, you want to ensure that any order IDs referenced in OrderItems exist in Orders. Similarly, any customers referred to in Orders must be present in the Customers table.

Although you can perform checks before inserting new rows (do a SELECT on another table to make sure the values are valid and present), it is best to avoid this practice for the following reasons:

- If database integrity rules are enforced at the client level, every client is obliged to enforce those rules—and inevitably some clients won't.

- You must also enforce the rules on UPDATE and DELETE operations.

- Performing client-side checks is a time-consuming process. Having the DBMS do the checks for you is far more efficient.

 Constraints Rules that govern how database data is inserted or manipulated.

DBMSs enforce referential integrity by imposing constraints on database tables. Most constraints are defined in table definitions (using the CREATE TABLE or ALTER TABLE as discussed in Lesson 17, "Creating and Manipulating Tables").

 Caution There are several different types of constraints, and each DBMS provides its own level of support for them. Therefore, the examples shown here might not work as is. Refer to your DBMS documentation before proceeding.

Primary Keys

I discussed primary keys briefly in Lesson 1, "Understanding SQL." A primary key is a special constraint that is used to ensure that values in a column (or set of columns) are unique and never change, in other words, a column (or columns) in a table whose values uniquely identify each row in the table. Primary key values uniquely identify every row in a table. This facilitates the direct manipulation of and interaction with individual rows. Without primary keys, it would be very difficult to safely UPDATE or DELETE specific rows without affecting any others.

Any column in a table can be established as the primary key, as long as it meets the following conditions:

- No two rows may have the same primary key value.

- Every row must have a primary key value. (Columns must not allow NULL values.)

- The column containing primary key values can never be modified or updated.

- Primary key values can never be reused. (If a row is deleted from the table, its primary key must not be assigned to any new rows.)

One way to define primary keys is at create time, as follows:

INPUT

```
CREATE TABLE Vendors
(
    vend_id         CHAR(10)     NOT NULL PRIMARY KEY,
    vend_name       CHAR(50)     NOT NULL,
    vend_address    CHAR(50)      NULL,
    vend_city       CHAR(50)     NULL,
    vend_state      CHAR         NULL,
    vend_zip        CHAR(10)     NULL
);
```

ANALYSIS In this example, the keyword PRIMARY KEY is added to the table definition so that vend_id becomes the primary key.

INPUT

```
ALTER TABLE Vendors
ADD CONSTRAINT PRIMARY KEY (vend_id)
```

ANALYSIS In this example, the same column is defined as the primary key, but the CONSTRAINT syntax is used instead. This syntax can be used both in CREATE TABLE and ALTER TABLE statements.

Foreign Keys

A foreign key is a column in a table whose values must be listed in a primary key in another table. Foreign keys are an extremely important part of ensuring referential integrity. To understand foreign keys, let's look at an example.

The Orders table contains a single row for each order entered into the system. Customer information is stored in the Customers table. Orders in Orders are tied to specific rows in the Customers table by customer ID. The customer ID is the primary key in the Customers table—each customer has a unique ID. The order number is the primary key in the Orders table—each order has a unique number.

The values in the customer ID column in the Orders table are not necessarily unique. If a customer has multiple orders, there will be multiple rows with the same customer ID (although each will have a different order number). But at the same time, the only values that are valid within the customer ID column in Orders are the IDs of customers in the Customers table.

That's what a foreign key does. In our example, a foreign key is defined on the Customer ID column in Orders so that the column can only accept values that are in the Customers table's primary key.

Here's one way to define this foreign key:

INPUT

```
CREATE TABLE Orders
(
    order_num       INTEGER           NOT NULL PRIMARY KEY,
    order_date      DATETIME      NOT NULL,
    cust_id         CHAR(10)       NOT NULL REFERENCES
Customers(cust_id)
);
```

ANALYSIS Here the table definition uses the REFERENCES keyword to state that any values in cust_id must be in cust_id in the Customers table.

The same thing could have been accomplished using CONSTRAINT syntax in an ALTER TABLE statement:

INPUT

```
CONSTRAINT FOREIGN KEY (cust_id) REFERNCES Customers (cust_id)
```

> **Foreign Keys Can Help Prevent Accidental Deletion**
> In addition to helping enforce referential integrity, foreign keys serve another invaluable purpose. After a foreign key is defined, your DBMS does not allow the deletion of rows that have related rows in other tables—for example, you are not allowed to delete a customer that has associated orders. The only way to delete that customer is to first delete the related orders (which in turn means deleting the related order items). Because they require such methodical deletion, foreign keys can help prevent the accidental deletion of data.

Unique Constraints

Unique constraints are used to ensure that all data in a column (or set of columns) is unique. They are similar to primary keys, but there are some important distinctions:

- A table can contain multiple unique constraints, but only one primary key is allowed per table.

- Unique constraint columns can contain NULL values.

- Unique constraint columns can be modified or updated.

- Unique constraint column values may never be reused.

- Unlike primary keys, unique constraints cannot be used to define foreign keys.

An example of the use of constraints is an employees table. Every employee has a unique social security number, but you would not want to use it for the primary key because it is too long (in addition to the fact that you might not want that information easily available). Therefore, every employee also has a unique employee ID (a primary key), in addition to his social security number.

Because the employee ID is a primary key, you can be sure that it is unique. You also might want the DBMS to ensure that each social security number is unique, too (to make sure that a typo does not result in the reuse of someone else's number). You can do this by defining a UNIQUE constraint on the social security number column.

The syntax for unique constraints is similar to that for other constraints. Either the UNIQUE keyword is defined in the table definition, or a separate CONSTRAINT is used.

Check Constraints

Check constraints are used to ensure that data in a column (or set of columns) meets a set of criteria that you specify. Common uses of this are

- Checking minimum or maximum values—for example, preventing an order of 0 items (even though 0 is a valid number)

- Specifying ranges—for example, making sure that a ship date is greater than or equal to today's date and not greater than a year from now

- Only allowing specific values—for example, only allowing M or F in a gender field

In other words, datatypes (discussed in Lesson 1) restrict the type of data that can be stored in a column. Check constraints place further restrictions within that datatype.

The following example applies a check constraint to our OrderItems table to ensure that all items have a quantity greater than 0:

INPUT

```
CREATE TABLE OrderItems
(
    order_num    INTEGER         NOT NULL,
    order_item   INTEGER          NOT NULL,
    prod_id      CHAR(10)      NOT NULL,
    quantity     INTEGER       NOT NULL    CHECK (quantity > 0),
    item_price   MONEY         NOT NULL
);
```

To check that a column named gender contains only M or F you can do the following in an ALTER TABLE statement:

INPUT

```
CONSTRAINT CHECK (gender LIKE '[MF]')
```

> **User-Defined Datatypes**   Some DBMSs allow you to define your own datatypes. These are essentially simple datatypes with check constraints (or other constraints) defined. So, for example, you can define your own datatype called gender that is a single character text datatype with a check constraint that restricts its values to M or F (and perhaps NULL for Unknown). The advantage of custom datatypes is that the constraints need only be applied once (in the datatype definition), and they are automatically applied each time the datatype is used. Check your DBMS documentation to determine if user-defined datatypes are supported.

Understanding Indexes

Indexes are used to logically sort data to improve the speed of searching and sorting operations. The best way to understand indexes is to envision the index at the back of a book (this book, for example).

Suppose you wanted to find all occurrences of the word *datatype* in this book. The simple way to do this would be to turn to page 1 and scan every line of every page looking for matches. Although that works, it is obviously not a workable solution. Scanning a few pages of text might be doable, but scanning an entire book in that manner is not. As the amount of text to be searched increases, so does the time it takes to pinpoint the desired data.

That is why books have indexes. An index is an alphabetical list of words with references to their locations in the book. To search for *datatype,* you find that word in the index to determine what pages it appears on. Then, you turn to those specific pages to find your matches.

What makes an index work? Simply, the fact that it is sorted correctly. The difficulty in finding words in a book is not the amount of content that must be searched; rather, it is the fact that the content is not sorted by word. If the content is sorted like a dictionary, an index is not needed (which is why dictionaries don't have indexes).

Database indexes work in much the same way. Primary key data is always sorted—that's just something the DBMS does for you. Retrieving specific rows by primary key is, therefore, always a fast and efficient operation.

Searching for values in other columns is usually not as efficient, however. For example, what if you want to retrieve all customers who live in a specific state? Because the table is not sorted by state, the DBMS must read every row in the table (starting at the very first row) looking for matches—just as you would have to do if you were trying to find words in a book without using an index.

The solution is to use an index. You may define an index on one or more columns so that the DBMS keeps a sorted list of the contents for its own use. After an index is defined, the DBMS uses it in much the same way as you would use a book index. It searches the sorted index to find the location of any matches, and then retrieves those specific rows.

But before you rush off to create dozens of indexes, bear in the mind the following:

- Indexes improve performance of retrieval operations, but they degrade the performance of data insertion, modification, and deletion. When these operations are executed, the DBMS has to dynamically update the index.

- Index data can take up lots of storage space.

- Not all data is suitable for indexing. Data that is not sufficiently unique (State, for example) will not benefit as much from indexing as data that has more possible values (first name or last name, for example).

- Indexes are used for data filtering and for data sorting. If you frequently sort data in a specific order, that order might be a candidate for indexing.

- Multiple columns can be defined in an index (for example, State plus City). Such an index will only be of use when data is sorted in State plus City order. (If you want to sort by City, this index would not be of any use.)

There is no hard and fast rule as to what should be indexed and when. Most DBMS provide utilities you can use to determine the effectiveness of indexes, and you should use these regularly.

Indexes are created with the CREATE INDEX statement (which varies dramatically from one DBMS to another). The following statement creates a simple index on the Products table's Product Name column:

INPUT

```
CREATE INDEX prod_name_ind
ON PRODUCTS (prod_name);
```

ANALYSIS   Every index must be uniquely named. Here the name prod_name_ind is defined after the keywords CREATE INDEX. ON is used to specify the table being indexed, and the columns to include in the index (just one in this example) are specified after the table name in parentheses.

> **Revisiting Indexes**   Index effectiveness changes as table data is added or changed. Many database administrators find that what once was an ideal set of indexes might not be so ideal after several months of data manipulation. It is always a good idea to revisit indexes on a regular basis to fine-tune them as needed.

Understanding Stored Procedures

Stored procedures are SQL statements that are stored on the DBMS server itself. Instead of entering SQL directly, you can call the stored procedure by name to execute the stored SQL. Stored procedures are invaluable for several reasons:

- Stored procedures execute more quickly than straight SQL statements because the code saved on the server is already parsed and ready for use.

- Stored procedures can contain multiple SQL operations. This enables you to call a single command and execute a set of statements (without having to specify them individually).

- Depending on the DBMS being used, stored procedures can return multiple result sets, as well as output parameters.

- Stored procedures can be used to hide complex data structures. Users can call the procedure, passing it values as needed, and it can manipulate tables internally as needed.

- Stored procedures can be used to secure underlying data. Users might not be given access to underlying tables (to prevent abuse or misuse). Instead they can communicate with a stored procedure, which, in turn, interacts with the underlying tables.

As you can see, there are lots of reasons to use stored procedures (and full coverage of the subject is beyond the scope of this book). Refer to your DBMS documentation for more details.

Understanding Triggers

Triggers are special stored procedures that are executed automatically when specific database activity occurs. Triggers might be associated with INSERT, UPDATE, and DELETE operations (or any combination thereof) on specific tables.

Unlike stored procedures (which are simply stored SQL statements), triggers are tied to individual tables. A trigger associated with INSERT operations on the Orders table will only be executed when a row is inserted into the Orders table. Similarly, a trigger on INSERT and UPDATE operations on the Customers table will only be executed when those specific operations occur on that table.

Within triggers, your code has access to the following:

- All new data in INSERT operations
- All new data and old data in UPDATE operations
- Deleted data in DELETE operations

Depending on the DBMS being used, triggers can be executed before or after a specified operation is performed.

Triggers have three primary uses:

- Ensuring data consistency—for example, converting all states to uppercase during INSERT or UPDATE operations

- Performing actions on other tables based on changes to a table— for example, writing an audit trail record to a log table each time a row is updated or deleted

- Performing additional validation and rolling back data if needed—for example, making sure a customer's available credit has not been exceeded and blocking the insertion if it has

- Calculating computed column values or update timestamps

As you probably expect by now, trigger creation syntax varies dramatically from one DBMS to another. Check your documentation for more details.

The following example creates a trigger that converts the cust_state on the Customers table field to uppercase on all INSERT and UPDATE operations. This is the SQL Server version:

INPUT

```
CREATE TRIGGER customer_state
ON Customers
FOR INSERT, UPDATE
AS
UPDATE Customers
SET cust_state = Upper(cust_state)
WHERE Customers.cust_id = inserted.cust_id;
```

This is the Oracle version:

INPUT

```
CREATE TRIGGER customer_state
AFTER INSERT UPDATE
FOR EACH ROW
BEGIN
UPDATE Customers
SET cust_state = Upper(cust_state)
WHERE Customers.cust_id = :OLD.cust_id
END;
```

Constrains Are Faster than Triggers As a rule, constraints are processed more quickly than triggers; so whenever possible, use constraints instead.

Summary

In this lesson, you learned how to use some advanced SQL features. Constraints are an important part of enforcing referential integrity; indexes can improve data retrieval performance; stored procedures can simplify SQL operations while providing additional functionality; lastly, triggers can be used to perform pre- or post-execution processing. Your own DBMS probably offers some form of these technologies, as well as others not mentioned here. I'd strongly suggest that you refer to your DBMS documentation for more details.

APPENDIX A

Sample Table Scripts

Writing SQL statements requires a good understanding of the underlying database design. Without knowing what information is stored in what table, how tables are related to each other, and the actual breakup of data within a row, it is impossible to write effective SQL.

You are strongly advised to actually try every example in every lesson in this book. All the lessons use a common set of data files. To assist you in better understanding the examples, and to enable you to follow along with the lessons, this appendix describes the tables used, their relationships, and how to build (or obtain) them.

Sample Tables Overview

The tables used throughout this book are part of an order entry system used by an imaginary distributor of toys. The tables are used to perform several tasks:

- Manage vendors
- Manage product catalogs
- Manage customer lists
- Enter customer orders

Making this all work requires five tables (that are closely interconnected as part of a relational database design). A description of each of the tables appears in the following sections.

Table Descriptions

What follows is a description of each of the five tables, along with the name of the columns within each table and their descriptions.

The VENDORS Table

The VENDORS table stores the vendors whose products are sold. Every vendor has a record in this table, and that vendor ID (the vend_id) column is used to match products with vendors.

TABLE A.1   VENDORS Table Columns

Column	Description
vend_id	Unique vendor ID
vend_name	Vendor name
vend_address	Vendor address
vend_city	Vendor city
vend_state	Vendor state
vend_zip	Vendor zip code

The PRODUCTS Table

The PRODUCTS table contains the product catalog, one product per row. Each product has a unique ID (the prod_id column) and is related to its vendor by vend_id (the vendor's unique ID).

TABLE A.2   PRODUCTS Table Columns

Column	Description
prod_id	Unique product ID
vend_id	Product vendor ID (relates to vend_id in VENDORS table)
prod_name	Product name
prod_price	Product price
prod_desc	Product description

The CUSTOMERS Table

The CUSTOMERS table stores all customer information. Each customer has a unique ID (the cust_id column).

TABLE A.3   CUSTOMERS Table Columns

Column	Description
cust_id	Unique customer ID
cust_name	Customer name
cust_address	Customer address
cust_city	Customer city
cust_state	Customer state
cust_zip	Customer zip code
cust_contact	Customer contact name
cust_email	Customer contact email address

The ORDERS Table

The ORDERS table stores customer orders (but not order details). Each order is uniquely numbered (the order_num column). Orders are associated with the appropriate customers by the cust_id column (which relates to the customer's unique ID in the CUSTOMERS table).

TABLE A.4 ORDERS Table Columns

Column	Description
order_num	Unique order number
order_date	Order date
cust_id	Order customer ID (relates to cust_id in CUSTOMERS table)

The ORDERITEMS Table

The ORDERITEMS table stores the actual items in each order, one row per item per order. For every row in ORDERS there are one or more rows in ORDERITEMS. Each order item is uniquely identified by the order number plus the order item (first item in order, second item in order, and so on). Order items are associated with their appropriate order by the order_num column (which relates to the order's unique ID in ORDERS). In addition, each order item contains the product ID of the item orders (which relates the item back to the PRODUCTS table).

TABLE A.5 ORDERITEMS Table Columns

Column	Description
order_num	Order number (relates to order_num in ORDERS table)
order_item	Order item number (sequential within an order)
prod_id	Product ID (relates to prod_id in PRODUCTS table)
quantity	Item quantity
item_price	Item price

Obtaining Sample Table and Scripts

In order to follow along with the examples, you need a set of populated tables. There are three ways to obtain tables for your own use:

- Manually create and populate the tables using the SQL statements below

- Download these same scripts from this book's Web page at http://www.forta.com/books/0672316641

- Download a fully populated Microsoft Access database (MDB file) from http://www.forta.com/books/0672316641

Obviously, downloading the scripts will save you time (and it will prevent you from introducing typos). Regardless of whether you plan to type the scripts manually or download them, please read the note below regarding script compatibility.

 Tip If you are planning on using Microsoft Access to follow along, you might want to download a fully created and populated MDB file.

If you plan to run the scripts yourself (either typed or downloaded), refer to Appendix B, "Working in Popular Applications," for instructions on running the scripts in your own environment.

Creating the Sample Tables

The following scripts can be used to create the five sample tables. Please note that these scripts have been designed for maximum compatibility among as many different DBMSs as possible. Because of this, the scripts are neither optimized nor complete. Each script is followed by notes that describe some changes or additions you may need (or want) to make.

> **Caution**   Please read the bulleted notes that appear
> after each script before actually executing it.

The VENDORS Table

INPUT

```
CREATE TABLE Vendors
(
    vend_id         CHAR(10)      NOT NULL,
    vend_name     CHAR(50)      NOT NULL,
    vend_address    CHAR(50)      ,
    vend_city     CHAR(50)     ,
    vend_state    CHAR          ,
    vend_zip     CHAR(10)
);
```

- All tables should have primary keys defined. This table should
  use vend_id as its primary key.

- If you are using Informix, explicitly state NULL for the
  vend_address, vend_city, vend_state, and vend_zip columns.

- DB2 users will need to specify where the table is to be created.

The PRODUCTS Table

INPUT

```
CREATE TABLE Products
(
    prod_id         CHAR(10)      NOT NULL,
    vend_id         CHAR(10)      NOT NULL,
    prod_name     CHAR(255)     NOT NULL,
    prod_price     DECIMAL(8,2)      NOT NULL,
    prod_desc     VARCHAR(1000)
);
```

- All tables should have primary keys defined. This table should
  use prod_id as its primary key.

- To enforce referential integrity, a foreign key should be defined
  on vend_id relating it to vend_id in VENDORS.

- If you are using Microsoft SQL Sever, Sybase, or Informix, you might want to use a datatype of MONEY instead of DECIMAL(8,2) for the prod_price column. DECIMAL(8,2) was used here because some DBMSs (most notably Oracle), do not support the MONEY datatype.

- If you are using Informix, explicitly state NULL for the prod_desc column.

- DB2 users will need to specify where the table is to be created.

The CUSTOMERS Table

INPUT

```
CREATE TABLE Customers
(
    cust_id         CHAR(10)     NOT NULL,
    cust_name     CHAR(50)     NOT NULL,
    cust_address    CHAR(50)      ,
    cust_city     CHAR(50)     ,
    cust_state    CHAR             ,
    cust_zip     CHAR(10)     ,
    cust_contact    CHAR(50)      ,
    cust_email    CHAR(255)
);
```

- All tables should have primary keys defined. This table should use cust_id as its primary key.

- If you are using Informix, explicitly state NULL for the cust_address, cust_city, cust_state, cust_zip, cust_contact, and cust_email columns.

- DB2 users will need to specify where the table is to be created.

The ORDERS Table

INPUT

```
CREATE TABLE Orders
(
    order_num    INTEGER         NOT NULL,
    order_date    DATETIME     NOT NULL,
```

```
    cust_id          CHAR(10)     NOT NULL
);
```

- All tables should have primary keys defined. This table should use order_num as its primary key.

- To enforce referential integrity, a foreign key should be defined on cust_id relating it to cust_id in CUSTOMERS.

- If you are using Oracle, change the order_date datatype from DATETIME to DATE.

- DB2 users will need to specify where the table is to be created.

The ORDERITEMS Table

```
CREATE TABLE OrderItems
(
    order_num       INTEGER          NOT NULL,
```

INPUT

```
    order_item      INTEGER          NOT NULL,
    prod_id          CHAR(10)    NOT NULL,
    quantity        INTEGER          NOT NULL,
    item_price      DECIMAL(8,2)     NOT NULL
);
```

- All tables should have primary keys defined. This table should use order_num and order_item as its primary keys.

- To enforce referential integrity, a foreign key should be defined on prod_id relating it to prod_id in PRODUCTS.

- If you are using Microsoft SQL Sever, Sybase, or Informix, you might want to use a datatype of MONEY, instead of DECIMAL(8,2), for the item_price column. DECIMAL(8,2) was used here because some DBMSs (most notably Oracle), do not support the MONEY datatype.

- DB2 users will need to specify where the table is to be created.

Populating the Sample Tables

The following scripts can be used to populate the sample tables.

> **Tip** If you have downloaded the populated Microsoft Access MDB file you will not have to run these scripts.

> **Caution** Do not run the following scripts more than once. If you have primary keys defined (and you should) then running these scripts a second time will generate SQL errors. If you do not have primary keys defined you'll end up with duplicate data (and your query results will not match those shown in the examples).

The VENDORS Table

`INPUT`

```
INSERT INTO Vendors(vend_id,
                    vend_name,
                    vend_address,
                    vend_city,
                    vend_state,
                    vend_zip)
VALUES('BRS01',
       'Bears R Us',
       '123 Main Street',
       'Bear Town',
       'MI',
       '44444');
INSERT INTO Vendors(vend_id,
                    vend_name,
                    vend_address,
                    vend_city,
                    vend_state,
                    vend_zip)
VALUES('BRE02',
```

```
            'Bear Emporium',
            '500 Park Street',
            'Anytown',
            'OH',
            '44333');
INSERT INTO Vendors(vend_id,
                    vend_name,
                    vend_address,
                    vend_city,
                    vend_state,
                    vend_zip)
VALUES('DLL01',
       'Doll House Inc.',
       '555 High Street',
       'Dollsville',
       'CA',
       '99999');
INSERT INTO Vendors(vend_id,
                    vend_name,
                    vend_address,
                    vend_city,
                    vend_state,
                    vend_zip)
VALUES('FRB01',
       'Furball Inc.',
       '1000 5th Avenue',
       'New York',
       'NY',
       '11111');
```

The PRODUCTS Table

INPUT

```
INSERT INTO Products(prod_id,
                     vend_id,
                     prod_name,
                     prod_price,
                     prod_desc)
VALUES('BR01',
       'BRS01',
       '8 inch teddy bear',
       5.99,
       '8 inch teddy bear, comes with cap and jacket');
INSERT INTO Products(prod_id,
```

```
                              vend_id,
                              prod_name,
                              prod_price,
                              prod_desc)
    VALUES('BR02',
           'BRS01',
           '12 inch teddy bear',
           8.99,
           '12 inch teddy bear, comes with cap and jacket');
    INSERT INTO Products(prod_id,
                              vend_id,
                              prod_name,
                              prod_price,
                              prod_desc)
    VALUES('BR03',
           'BRS01',
           '18 inch teddy bear',
           11.99,
           '18 inch teddy bear, comes with cap and jacket');
    INSERT INTO Products(prod_id,
                              vend_id,
                              prod_name,
                              prod_price,
                              prod_desc)
    VALUES('BNBG01',
           'DLL01',
           'Fish bean bag toy',
           3.49,
           'Fish bean bag toy, complete with bean bag worms with
           ➥which to feed it');
           INSERT INTO Products(prod_id,
                              vend_id,
                              prod_name,
                              prod_price,
                              prod_desc)
    VALUES('BNBG02',
           'DLL01',
           'Bird bean bag toy',
           3.49,
           'Bird bean bag toy, eggs are not included');
    INSERT INTO Products(prod_id,
                              vend_id,
                              prod_name,
                              prod_price,
                              prod_desc)
    VALUES('BNBG03',
           'DLL01',
```

```
          'Rabbit bean bag toy',
          3.49,
          'Rabbit bean bag toy, comes with bean bag carrots');
INSERT INTO Products(prod_id,
                     vend_id,
                     prod_name,
                     prod_price,
                     prod_desc)
VALUES('RGAN01',
       'DLL01',
       'Raggedy Ann',
       4.99,
       '18 inch Raggedy Ann doll');
```

The CUSTOMERS Table

INPUT

```
INSERT INTO Customers(cust_id,
                      cust_name,
                      cust_address,
                      cust_city,
                      cust_state,
                      cust_zip,
                      cust_contact,
                      cust_email)
VALUES('1000000001',
       'Village Toys',
       '200 Maple Lane',
       'Detroit',
       'MI',
       '44444',
       'John Smith',
       'sales@villagetoys.com');
INSERT INTO Customers(cust_id,
                      cust_name,
                      cust_address,
                      cust_city,
                      cust_state,
                      cust_zip,
                      cust_contact,
                      cust_email)
VALUES('1000000002',
       'Kids Place',
       '333 South Lake Drive',
       'Columbus',
```

```
            'OH',
            '43333',
            'Michelle Green');
INSERT INTO Customers(cust_id,
                          cust_name,
                          cust_address,
                          cust_city,
                          cust_state,
                          cust_zip,
                          cust_contact,
                          cust_email)
VALUES('1000000003',
        'Fun4All',
        '1 Sunny Place',
        'Muncie',
        'IN',
        '42222',
        'Jim Jones',
        'jjones@fun4all.com');
INSERT INTO Customers(cust_id,
                          cust_name,
                          cust_address,
                          cust_city,
                          cust_state,
                          cust_zip,
                          cust_contact,
                          cust_email)
VALUES('1000000004',
        'Fun4All',
        '829 Riverside Drive',
        'Phoenix',
        'AZ',
        '88888',
        'Denise L. Stephens',
        'dstephens@fun4all.com');
INSERT INTO Customers(cust_id,
                          cust_name,
                          cust_address,
                          cust_city,
                          cust_state,
                          cust_zip,
                          cust_contact,
                          cust_email)
```

```
VALUES('1000000005',
       'The Toy Store',
       '4545 53rd Street',
       'Chicago',
       'IL',
       '54545',
       'Kim Howard');
```

The ORDERS Table

`INPUT`

```
INSERT INTO Orders(order_num,
                   order_date,
                   cust_id)
VALUES(20005,
       '1999/5/1',
       '1000000001');
INSERT INTO Orders(order_num,
                   order_date,
                   cust_id)
VALUES(20006,
       '1999/1/12',
       '1000000003');
INSERT INTO Orders(order_num,
                   order_date,
                   cust_id)
VALUES(20007,
       '1999/1/30',
       '1000000004');
INSERT INTO Orders(order_num,
                   order_date,
                   cust_id)
VALUES(20008,
       '1999/2/3',
       '1000000005');
INSERT INTO Orders(order_num,
                   order_date,
                   cust_id)
VALUES(20009,
       '1999/2/8',
       '1000000001');
```

The **ORDERITEMS** Table

```
INSERT INTO OrderItems(order_num,
                       order_item,
                       prod_id,
                       quantity,
                       item_price)
VALUES(20005,
       1,
       'BR01',
       100,
       5.49);
INSERT INTO OrderItems(order_num,
                       order_item,
                       prod_id,
                       quantity,
                       item_price)
VALUES(20005,
       2,
       'BR03',
       100,
       10.99);
INSERT INTO OrderItems(order_num,
                       order_item,
                       prod_id,
                       quantity,
                       item_price)
VALUES(20006,
       1,
       'BR01',
       20,
       5.99);
INSERT INTO OrderItems(order_num,
                       order_item,
                       prod_id,
                       quantity,
                       item_price)
VALUES(20006,
       2,
       'BR02',
       10,
       8.99);
INSERT INTO OrderItems(order_num,
                       order_item,
                       prod_id,
                       quantity,
                       item_price)
```

```
VALUES(20006,
       3,
       'BR03',
       10,
       11.99);
INSERT INTO OrderItems(order_num,
                       order_item,
                       prod_id,
                       quantity,
                       item_price)
VALUES(20007,
       1,
       'BR03',
       50,
       11.49);
INSERT INTO OrderItems(order_num,
                       order_item,
                       prod_id,
                       quantity,
                       item_price)
VALUES(20007,
       2,
       'BNBG01',
       100,
       2.99);
INSERT INTO OrderItems(order_num,
                       order_item,
                       prod_id,
                       quantity,
                       item_price)
VALUES(20007,
       3,
       'BNBG02',
       100,
       2.99);
INSERT INTO OrderItems(order_num,
                       order_item,
                       prod_id,
                       quantity,
                       item_price)
VALUES(20007,
       4,
       'BNBG03',
       100,
       2.99);
INSERT INTO OrderItems(order_num,
                       order_item,
```

```
                               prod_id,
                               quantity,
                               item_price)
VALUES(20007,
       5,
       'RGAN01',
       50,
       4.49);
INSERT INTO OrderItems(order_num,
                               order_item,
                               prod_id,
                               quantity,
                               item_price)
VALUES(20008,
       1,
       'RGAN01',
       5,
       4.99);
INSERT INTO OrderItems(order_num,
                               order_item,
                               prod_id,
                               quantity,
                               item_price)
VALUES(20008,
       2,
       'BR03',
       5,
       11.99);
INSERT INTO OrderItems(order_num,
                               order_item,
                               prod_id,
                               quantity,
                               item_price)
VALUES(20008,
       3,
       'BNBG01',
       10,
       3.49);
INSERT INTO OrderItems(order_num,
                               order_item,
                               prod_id,
                               quantity,
                               item_price)
VALUES(20008,
       4,
       'BNBG02',
       10,
```

```
        3.49);
INSERT INTO OrderItems(order_num,
                       order_item,
                       prod_id,
                       quantity,
                       item_price)
VALUES(20008,
       5,
       'BNBG03',
       10,
       3.49);
INSERT INTO OrderItems(order_num,
                       order_item,
                       prod_id,
                       quantity,
                       item_price)
VALUES(20009,
       1,
       'BNBG01',
       250,
       2.49);
INSERT INTO OrderItems(order_num,
                       order_item,
                       prod_id,
                       quantity,
                       item_price)
VALUES(20009,
       2,
       'BNBG02',
       250,
       2.49);
INSERT INTO OrderItems(order_num,
                       order_item,
                       prod_id,
                       quantity,
                       item_price)
VALUES(20009,
       3,
       'BNBG03',
       250,
       2.49);
```

Appendix B

Working in Popular Applications

As explained in Lesson 1, "Understanding SQL," SQL is not an application; it is a language. To follow along with the examples in this book, you need an application that supports the execution of SQL statements.

This appendix describes the steps for executing SQL statements in some of the more commonly used applications.

Configuring ODBC Data Sources

Many of the applications described below use ODBC for database integration, and so we'll start with a brief overview of ODBC and instructions for configuring ODBC Data Sources.

ODBC is a standard that is used to enable clients' applications to interact with different backend databases or underlying database engines. Using ODBC, is it possible to write code in one client (for example, Microsoft Query, Allaire ColdFusion, or Seagate Crystal Reports) and have those tools interact with almost any database or DBMS.

ODBC itself is not a database. Rather, ODBC is a wrapper around databases that makes all databases behave in a consistent and clearly defined fashion. It accomplishes this by using software drivers that have two primary functions. First, they encapsulate any native database features or peculiarities and hide these from the client. Second, they provide a common language for interacting with these databases (performing translations when needed). The language used by ODBC is SQL.

ODBC client applications do not interact with databases directly. Instead, they interact with ODBC Data Sources. A Data Source is a logical database that includes the driver (each database type has its own driver) and information on how to connect to the database (file paths, serve names, and so forth).

After ODBC Data Sources are defined, any ODBC-compliant application can use them. ODBC Data Sources are not application specific; they are system specific.

> **ODBC Differences** There are many different versions of the ODBC applet, making it impossible to provide exact instructions that would apply to all versions. Pay close attention to the prompts when setting up your own Data Sources.

ODBC Data Sources are defined using the Windows Control Panel's ODBC applet. To set up an ODBC Data Source do the following:

1. Open the Windows Control Panel's ODBC applet.

2. Most ODBC Data Sources should be set up to be system-wide Data Sources (as opposed to user-specific Data Sources), so select System DSN, if that option is available to you.

3. Click the Add button to add a new Data Source.

4. Select the driver to use. There is usually a default set of drivers that provides support for major Microsoft products. Other drivers might be installed on your system. You must select a driver that matches the type of database to which you'll be connecting.

5. Depending on the type of database or DBMS, you are prompted for server name or file path information and possibly login information. Provide this information as requested and then follow the rest of the prompts to create the Data Source.

Using Allaire ColdFusion

Allaire's ColdFusion is a Web-application development platform. ColdFusion uses a tag-based language to create scripts. To test your SQL, create a simple page that you can execute by calling it from your Web browser. Perform the following steps:

1. ColdFusion uses OBDC to interact with databases, so an ODBC Data Source must be present before proceeding (see the earlier instructions). The ColdFusion Administrator program also provides an optional Web-based interface to define ODBC Data Sources.

2. Create a new ColdFusion page (with a CFM extension) using ColdFusion Studio, HomeSite, or any other text editor.

3. Use the CFML `<CFQUERY>` and `</CFQUERY>` tags to create a query block. Name it using the `NAME` attribute and define the Data Source in the `DATASOURCE` attribute.

4. Type your SQL statement between the `<CFQUERY>` and `</CFQUERY>` tags.

5. Use a `<CFOUTPUT>` loop to display the query results.

6. Save the page in any executable directory beneath the Web server root.

7. Execute the page by calling it from a Web browser.

Using DB2

IBM's DB2 is a powerful high-end, multi-platform DBMS. It comes with a whole suite of client tools that may be used to execute SQL statements. The instructions that follow use the Query Management Facility (or QMF) utility because it is one of the simplest and most versatile of the bundled applications:

1. Select QMF from the ISPF menu.

2. To create a new query, press F6 to access the QMF Query panel.

3. Enter the SQL statement and press F2 to execute it. The results will be displayed on the screen.

4. QMF also enables you to specify different formatting and output options. Press F9 to access the report form screen.

Using Informix Dynamic Server 7.x

Informix's Dynamic Server is available for several different operating systems, and the exact sequence of steps to execute SQL varies from one platform to the next. The following instructions are for the Windows NT version of Informix Dynamic Server. You might have to adapt the steps slightly for other platforms. To use the Informix SQL Editor, do the following:

1. Launch the Informix Enterprise Command Center (also known as IECC).

2. Select SQL Editor from the Tools menu.

3. Select a server and database from the drop-down list box at the top-right of the screen.

4. Provide user name and password for authentication when prompted.

5. Type your SQL in the edit area beneath the SQL tab. (There might only be one tab at this point; other tabs will be displayed as needed.)

6. Click the Execute button to execute the SQL statement.

7. Results will be displayed in the Output tab.

Using Microsoft Access

Microsoft Access is used interactively to create and manage databases and to interact and manipulate data. A frequently overlooked feature in the Access Query designer lets you specify SQL for direct execution. This enables you to use Access to send SQL statements to any ODBC Data Source. To use this feature, do the following:

1. Microsoft Access uses OBDC to interact with databases, so an ODBC Data Source must be present before proceeding (see the earlier instructions).

2. Launch Microsoft Access. You will be prompted to open (or create) a database. Open any database.

3. Select Queries in the Database window. Then click on the New button and select Design View.

4. You'll be prompted with a Show Table dialog. Close that window without selecting any tables.

5. From the Query menu, select SQL Specific and then select SQL Pass-Through.

6. From the View menu, select Properties to display the Query Properties dialog.

7. Click in the ODBC Connect Str field and then click the ... button to display the Select Data Source dialog, which you can use to select the ODBC Data Source.

8. Select your Data Source and click OK to return to the Query Properties dialog.

9. Click on the Returns Records field. If you are executing a SELECT statement (or any statement that returns results), set Returns Records to Yes. If you are executing a SQL statement that does not return data (for example, INSERT, UPDATE, or DELETE) set Return Records to No.

10. Type your SQL statement in the SQL Pass-Through Query window.

11. To execute the SQL statement click on the Run button (the one with the red exclamation mark).

Using Microsoft ASP

Microsoft ASP is a scripting language for creating Web-based applications. To test your SQL statements within an ASP page, you must create a page that you can execute by calling it from your Web browser. Here are the steps need to execute a SQL statement within an ASP page:

1. ASP uses OBDC to interact with databases, so an ODBC Data Source must be present before proceeding (see the earlier instructions).

2. Create a new ASP page (with an ASP extension) using any text editor.

3. Use `Server.CreateObject` to create an instance of the `ADODB.Connection` object.

4. Use the `Open` method to open the desired ODBC Data Source.

5. Pass your SQL statement to a call to the `Execute` method. The `Execute` method returns a result set. Use a `Set` command to save the result returned into a result set.

6. To display the results, you must loop through the retrieved data using a `<% Do While NOT EOF %>` loop.

7. Save the page in any executable directory beneath the Web server root.

8. Execute the page by calling it from a Web browser.

Using Microsoft Query

Microsoft Query is a standalone SQL query tool and is an ideal utility for testing SQL statements against ODBC Data Sources. Microsoft Query is optionally installed with other Microsoft products (for example, Microsoft Office), as well as with other third-party products. To use Microsoft Query, do the following:

1. Microsoft Query uses OBDC to interact with databases, so an ODBC Data Source must be present before you can proceed (see the earlier instructions).

2. Before you can use Microsoft Query, it must be installed on your computer. Browse your program groups beneath the Start button to locate it. If it is not present under the Start button, use Start Find to locate it on your system. (It is often present without your knowing it.) The files to look for are `MSQRY32.EXE` or `MSQUERY.EXE`.

3. From the File menu, select Execute SQL to display the Execute SQL window.

4. Click the Data Sources button to select the desired ODBC Data Source. If the Data Source you need is not listed, click Other to locate it. After you have selected the correct Data Source, click the Use button.

5. Type your SQL statement in the SQL Statement box.

6. Click Execute to execute the SQL statement and to display any returned data.

Using Microsoft SQL Server 6.x

Microsoft SQL Server 6 and 6.5 feature a Windows-based interactive SQL application called iSQL/W, which is ideal for testing and experimenting with SQL statements. To use iSQL/W, do the following:

1. Launch the iSQL/W application (from the Microsoft SQL Server 6 or Microsoft SQL Server 6.5 program group).

2. You'll be prompted for server and login information. Log in to your SQL Server (starting the server if appropriate).

3. When the query screen is displayed, select the database from the drop-down DB list box.

4. Type your SQL in the large text window, and then click the Execute Query button (the one with the green arrow) to execute it. (You can also click Ctrl+E or select Execute from the Query menu.)

5. The results will be displayed in a separate pane beneath the SQL window.

Using Microsoft SQL Server 7

Microsoft SQL Server 7 features a Windows-based query analysis tool called Query Analyzer. Although this tool is primarily designed to analyze SQL statement execution and optimization, it does present an ideal environment for testing and experimenting with SQL statements. Here's how to use the Query Analyzer:

1. Launch the Query Analyzer application (from the Microsoft SQL Server 7.0 program group).

2. You'll be prompted for server and login information. Log in to your SQL Server (starting the server if appropriate).

3. When the query screen is displayed, select the database from the drop-down DB list box.

4. Type your SQL in the large text window, and then click the Execute Query button (the one with the green arrow) to execute it. (You can also click F5 or select Execute from the Query menu.)

5. The results will be displayed in a separate pane beneath the SQL window.

Using Microsoft Visual Basic

Microsoft Visual Basic 6 provides tools and components for building database client applications. But rather than building an entire application to test your SQL, VB6 includes a Visual Database Manager that can be used to directly test and execute SQL statements. To use the Visual Database Manager do the following:

1. Microsoft Visual Basic uses ODBC (and DAO) for database integration. To interact with ODBC, an ODBC Data Source must be present before proceeding (see the earlier instructions).

2. Launch the Visual Basic Development Environment.

3. Select Visual Database Manager from the Add-Ins menu.

4. From the File menu, select Open Database and then select ODBC.

5. Select the ODBC Data Source to connect to. You might be prompted for a login and password (depending on the DBMS you are trying to use).

6. After you have connected to a Data Source, you'll be able to type SQL directly into the SQL Statement Window. Type your SQL statement and then click the Execute button.

Using Microsoft Visual C++

Microsoft Visual C++ provides no mechanism for direct execution (and reporting) of SQL statements. But it does provide MFC classes that can be used to database-enable Windows applications. To use these classes, you should be familiar with MFC and MSVC's AppWizard and ClassWizard. To use these classes, do the following:

1. Microsoft Visual C++ provides MFC classes that encapsulate ODBC (and DAO) integration. To interact with ODBC, an ODBC Data Source must be present before proceeding. (See the earlier instructions.)

2. To support the use of ODBC calls, your MFC application must have database support enabled. This option may be selected in the app wizard. (If you are using Visual C++ Enterprise Edition, you can also create a direct database project.)

3. You'll need a CRecordset class to actually submit the SQL and return results. CRecordset class members can be used to specify SQL statement clauses.

4. MSVC's AppWizard and ClassWizard are then used to bind columns to selected tables in your recordset.

5. The CRecordView class can be derived to create a form to display the SQL results.

Using Oracle 8

Oracle 8 has a management tool called Enterprise Manager. One of the tools in Enterprise Manager is the SQL Worksheet, which enables you to manually enter SQL for execution. Here's how to use this tool:

1. Launch Oracle Enterprise Manager, and select SQL Worksheet.

2. You'll be prompted for login information. Provide a user name and password and connect to the database server.

3. The SQL Worksheet screen is divided into two panes. Type your SQL in the lower pane.

4. To execute the SQL statement, click the Execute button (the one with the picture of the lightning bolt). Results will be displayed in the upper pane.

Using Sybase

Sybase SQL Server is very similar to Microsoft SQL Server (prior to version 7), and they share many of the same tools and utilities. One command line utility that is available in every Sybase installation is iSQL (which is also included with Microsoft SQL Server). To use iSQL, do the following:

1. Execute the iSQL application. (It is a command line application that resides in the Sybase directory.) You must specify a login name using the -U parameter, a password using the -P parameter, and a server name using the -S parameter.

2. You'll be prompted with a 1>. This is the first line on which you type your SQL statement. (You may type the SQL on one line or broken over many lines.)

3. Keep typing your SQL statement, pressing Enter at the end of each line. The line number will increment by one each time you do so.

4. Type GO on a new line and press Enter to execute your SQL.

5. The results will be displayed on the screen. (To redirect output to a file, use the iSQL -0 attribute.)

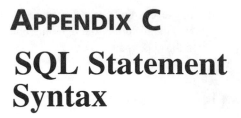

APPENDIX C
SQL Statement Syntax

To help you find the syntax you need when you need it, this appendix lists the syntax for the most frequently used SQL operations. Each statement starts with a brief description and then displays the appropriate syntax. For added convenience, you'll also find cross references to the lessons where specific statements are taught.

When reading statement syntax, remember the following:

- The ¦ symbol is used to indicate one of several options, so NULL¦NOT NULL means specify either NULL or NOT NULL.

- Keywords or clauses contained within square parentheses [like this] are optional.

- The syntax listed below will work with almost all DBMSs. You are advised to consult your own DBMS documentation for details of implementing specific syntactical changes.

ALTER TABLE

ALTER TABLE is used to update the schema of an existing table. To create a new table, use CREATE TABLE. See Lesson 17, "Creating and Manipulating Tables," for more information.

```
ALTER TABLE tablename
(
    ADD¦DROP    column    datatype    [NULL¦NOT NULL] [CONSTRAINTS],
    ADD¦DROP    column    datatype    [NULL¦NOT NULL] [CONSTRAINTS],
    ...
);
```

COMMIT

COMMIT is used to write a transaction to the database. See Lesson 19,
"Using Transaction Processing," for more information.

```
COMMIT [TRANSACTION];
```

CREATE INDEX

CREATE INDEX is used to create an index on one or more columns. See
Lesson 20, "Using Advanced SQL Features," for more information.

```
CREATE INDEX indexname
ON tablename (column, ...);
```

CREATE TABLE

CREATE TABLE is used to create new database tables. To update the schema
of an existing table, use ALTER TABLE. See Lesson 17, "Creating and
Manipulating Tables," for more information.

```
CREATE TABLE tablename
(
    column      datatype      [NULL|NOT NULL]      [CONSTRAINTS],
    column      datatype      [NULL|NOT NULL]      [CONSTRAINTS],
    ...
);
```

CREATE VIEW

CREATE VIEW is used to create a new view of one or more tables. See
Lesson 18, "Using Views," for more information.

```
CREATE VIEW viewname AS
SELECT columns, ...
FROM tables, ...
[WHERE ...]
[GROUP BY ...]
[HAVING ...];
```

DELETE

DELETE deletes one or more rows from a table. See Lesson 16, "Updating and Deleting Data," for more information.

```
DELETE FROM tablename
[WHERE ...];
```

DROP

DROP permanently removes database objects (tables, views, indexes, and so forth). See Lesson 17, "Creating and Manipulating Tables," and Lesson 18, "Using Views," for more information.

```
DROP INDEX¦TABLE¦VIEW indexname¦tablename¦viewname;
```

INSERT

INSERT adds a single row to a table. See Lesson 15, "Inserting Data," for more information.

```
INSERT INTO tablename [(columns, ...)]
VALUES(values, ...);
```

INSERT SELECT

INSERT SELECT inserts the results of a SELECT into a table. See Lesson 15, "Inserting Data," for more information.

```
INSERT INTO tablename [(columns, ...)]
SELECT columns, ... FROM tablename, ...
[WHERE ...];
```

ROLLBACK

ROLLBACK is used to undo a transaction block. See Lesson 19, "Using Transaction Processing," for more information.

```
ROLLBACK [ TO savepointname];
```

Or

```
ROLLBACK TRANSACTION;
```

SELECT

SELECT is used to retrieve data from one or more tables (or views). See Lesson 2, "Retrieving Data;" Lesson 3, "Sorting Retrieved Data;" and Lesson 4, "Filtering Data," for more basic information. (Lessons 2–14 all cover aspects of SELECT.)

```
SELECT columnname, ...
FROM tablename, ...
[WHERE ...]
[GROUP BY ...]
[HAVING ...]
[ORDER BY ...];
```

UPDATE

UPDATE updates one or more rows in a table. See Lesson 16, "Updating and Deleting Data," for more information.

```
UPDATE tablename
SET columnname = value, ...
[WHERE …];
```

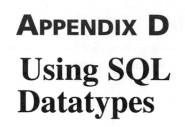

APPENDIX D

Using SQL Datatypes

As explained in Lesson 1, "Understanding SQL," datatypes are basically rules that define what data may be stored in a column and how that data is actually stored.

Datatypes are used for several reasons:

- Datatypes enable you to restrict the type of data that can be stored in a column. For example, a numeric datatype column will only accept numeric values.

- Datatypes allow for more efficient storage, internally. Numbers and date time values can be stored in a more condensed format than text strings.

- Datatypes allow for alternate sorting orders. If everything is treated as strings, 1 comes before 10, which comes before 2. (Strings are sorted in dictionary sequence, one character at a time starting from the left.) As numeric datatypes, the numbers would be sorted correctly.

When designing tables, pay careful attention to the datatypes being used. Using the wrong datatype can seriously impact your application. Changing the datatypes of existing populated columns is not a trivial task. (In addition, doing so can result in data loss.)

Although this lesson is by no means a complete tutorial on datatypes and how they are to be used, it explains the major datatype types, what they are used for, and compatibility issues that you should be aware of.

No Two DBMSs Are Exactly Alike   Unfortunately, datatypes can vary dramatically from one DBMS to the next. Even the same datatype name can mean different things to different DBMSs. Be sure you consult your DBMS documentation for details on exactly what it supports and how.

String Datatypes

The most commonly used datatypes are string datatypes. These store strings: for example, names, addresses, phone numbers, and zip codes. There are basically two types of string datatype that you can use—fixed-length strings and variable-length strings (see Table D.1).

Fixed length strings are datatypes that are defined to accept a fixed number of characters, and that number is specified when the table is created. For example, you might allow 30 characters in a first-name column or 11 characters in a social-security-number column (the exact number needed allowing for the two dashes). Fixed-length columns do not allow more than the specified number of characters. They also allocate storage space for as many characters as specified. So, if the string Ben is stored in a 30-character first-name field, a full 30 characters are stored (and the text is padded with spaces or nulls as needed).

Variable-length strings store text of any length (the maximum varies by datatype and DBMS). Some variable-length datatypes have a fixed-length minimum. Others are entirely variable. Either way, only the data specified is saved (and no extra data is stored).

If variable-length datatypes are so flexible, why would you ever want to used fixed-length datatypes? The answer is performance. DBMSs can sort and manipulate fixed-length columns far more quickly than they can sort variable-length columns. In addition, many DBMSs will not allow you to index variable-length columns. This also dramatically impacts performance. (See Lesson 20, "Using Advanced SQL Features," for more information on indexes.)

TABLE D.1   String Datatypes

Datatype	Description
CHAR	Fixed length string from 1 to 255 chars long. Its size must be specified at create time.
NCHAR	Special form of CHAR designed to support multibyte or Unicode characters. (The exact specifications vary dramatically from one implementation to the next.)
NVARCHAR	Special form of TEXT designed to support multibyte or Unicode characters. (Exact specifications vary dramatically from one implementation to the next.)
TEXT (also called LONG or MEMO or VARCHAR)	Variable-length text.

Using Quotes   Regardless of the form of string datatype being used, string values must always be surrounded by single quotes.

When Numeric Values Are Not Numeric Values   You might think that phone numbers and zip codes should be stored in numeric fields (after all, they only store numeric data), but doing so would not be advisable. If you store the zip code 01234 in a numeric field, the number 1234 would be saved. You'd actually lose a digit.

The basic rule to follow is: If the number is a number used in calculations (sums, averages, and so on), it belongs in a numeric datatype column. If it is used as a literal string (that happens to contain only digits), it belongs in a string datatype column.

Numeric Datatypes

Numeric datatypes store numbers. Most DBMSs support multiple numeric datatypes, each with a different range of numbers that can be stored in it. Obviously, the larger the supported range, the more storage space needed. In addition, some numeric datatypes support the use of decimal points (and fractional numbers) whereas others support only whole numbers. Table D.2 lists common uses for various datatypes, not all DBMSs follow the exact naming conventions and descriptions listed here.

TABLE D.2   Numeric Datatypes

Datatype	Description
BIT	Single bit value, either 0 or 1, used primarily for on/off flags
DECIMAL (also called NUMERIC)	Fixed or floating point values with varying levels of precision
FLOAT (also called NUMBER)	Floating point values
INT (also called INTEGER)	4-byte integer value that supports numbers from –2147483648 to 2147483647
REAL	4-byte floating point values
SMALLINT	2-byte integer value that supports numbers from –32768 to 32767
TINYINT	1-byte integer value that supports numbers from 0 to 255

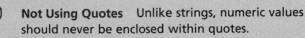

Not Using Quotes   Unlike strings, numeric values should never be enclosed within quotes.

> **Currency Datatypes**   Most DBMSs (Oracle is the notable exception) support a special numeric datatype for storing monetary values. Usually called MONEY or CURRENCY, these datatypes are essentially DECIMAL datatypes with specific ranges that make them well-suited for storing currency values.

Date and Time Datatypes

All DBMSs support datatypes designed for the storage of date and time values (see Table D.3). Like numeric values, most DBMSs support multiple datatypes, each with different ranges and levels of precision.

TABLE D.3   Numeric Datatypes

Datatype	Description
DATE	Date value
DATETIME (also known as TIMESTAMP)	Date time values
SMALLDATETIME	Date time values with accuracy to the minute (no seconds or milliseconds)

> **Specifying Dates**   There is no standard way to define a date that will be understood by every DBMS. Most implementations understand formats like 1999-12-30 or Dec 30th, 1999, but even those can be problematic to some DBMSs. Make sure to consult your DBMS documentation for a list of the date formats that it will recognize.

> **ODBC Dates** Because every DBMS has its own format for specifying dates, ODBC created a format of its own that will work with every database when ODBC is being used. The ODBC format looks like {d '1999-12-30'} for dates, {t '21:46:29'} for times, and {ts '1999-12-30 21:46:29'} for date time values. If you are using SQL via ODBC, be sure your dates and times are formatted in this fashion.

Binary Datatypes

Binary datatypes are some of the least compatible (and, fortunately, also some of the least used) datatypes. Unlike all the datatypes explained thus far, which have very specific uses, binary datatypes can contain any data, even binary information, such as graphic images, multimedia, and word processor documents (see Table D.4).

TABLE D.4 Binary Datatypes

Datatype	Description
BINARY	Fixed-length binary data (maximum length varies from 255 bytes to 8,000 bytes, depending on implementation)
LONG RAW	Variable-length binary data up to 2GB
RAW (called BINARY by some implementations)	Fixed-length binary data up to 255 bytes
VARBINARY	Variable-length binary data (maximum length varies from 255 bytes to 8,000 bytes, depending on implementation)

APPENDIX E

SQL Reserved Words

SQL is a language made up of keywords—special words that are used in performing SQL operations. Special care must be taken to not use these keywords when naming databases, tables, columns, and any other database objects. Thus, these keywords are considered reserved.

This appendix contains a list of the more common reserved words found in major DBMSs. Please note the following:

- Keywords tend to be very DBMS-specific, and not all the keywords that follow are used by all DBMSs.

- Many DBMSs have extended the list of SQL reserved words to include terms specific to their implementations. Most DBMS-specific keywords are not listed in the following section.

- To ensure future compatibility and portability, it is a good idea to avoid any and all reserved words, even those not reserved by your own DBMS.

ABSOLUTE	ANY	AUTOINC
ACTION	ARE	AVG
ACTIVE	AS	BACKUP
ADD	ASC	BEFORE
AFTER	ASCENDING	BEGIN
ALL	ASSERTION	BETWEEN
ALLOCATE	AT	BIT
ALTER	AUTHORIZATION	BLOB
AND	AUTO	BOOLEAN

BOTH	CONDITIONAL	DEC
BREAK	CONFIRM	DECIMAL
BROWSE	CONNECT	DECLARE
BULK	CONNECTION	DEFAULT
BY	CONSTRAINT	DELETE
BYTES	CONSTRAINTS	DENY
CACHE	CONTAINING	DESC
CASCADE	CONTAINS	DESCENDING
CASCADED	CONTAINSTABLE	DESCRIBE
CASE	CONTINUE	DISCONNECT
CAST	CONTROLROW	DISK
CATALOG	CONVERT	DISTINCT
CHAR	COUNT	DISTRIBUTED
CHARACTER	CREATE	DO
CHECK	CROSS	DOMAIN
CHECKPOINT	CSTRING	DOUBLE
CLOSE	CUBE	DROP
CLUSTERED	CURRENT	DUMMY
COALESCE	CURSOR	DUMP
COLLATE	DATABASE	ELSE
COLUMN	DATE	END
COMMENT	DATETIME	ERRLVL
COMMIT	DAY	ERROREXIT
COMMITTED	DBCC	ESCAPE
COMPUTE	DEALLOCATE	EXCEPT
COMPUTED	DEBUG	EXCEPTION

EXEC	GROUP	LEFT
EXECUTE	HAVING	LENGTH
EXISTS	HOLDLOCK	LEVEL
EXIT	HOUR	LIKE
EXTERNAL	IDENTITY	LINENO
EXTRACT	IF	LOAD
FALSE	IN	LOCAL
FETCH	INACTIVE	LOGFILE
FILE	INDEX	LONG
FILLFACTOR	INDICATOR	LOWER
FILTER	INNER	MANUAL
FLOAT	INPUT	MATCH
FLOPPY	INSERT	MAX
FOR	INT	MERGE
FOREIGN	INTEGER	MESSAGE
FOUND	INTERSECT	MIN
FREETEXT	INTERVAL	MINUTE
FREETEXTTABLE	INTO	MIRROREXIT
FROM	IS	MODULE
FULL	ISOLATION	MONEY
FUNCTION	JOIN	MONTH
GENERATOR	KEY	NAMES
GET	KILL	NATIONAL
GO	LANGUAGE	NATURAL
GOTO	LAST	NCHAR
GRANT	LEADING	NEXT

NO	PARTIAL	RESERV
NOCHECK	PASSWORD	RESERVING
NONCLUSTERED	PERCENT	RESTORE
NONE	PERM	RESTRICT
NOT	PERMANENT	RETAIN
NULL	PIPE	RETURN
NULLIF	PLAN	RETURNS
NUMERIC	POSITION	REVOKE
OF	PRECISION	RIGHT
OFF	PREPARE	ROLLBACK
OFFSETS	PRIMARY	ROLLUP
ON	PRINT	RULE
ONCE	PRIOR	SAVE
ONLY	PRIVILEGES	SCHEMA
OPEN	PROC	SECOND
OPTION	PROCEDURE	SECTION
OR	PROCESSEXIT	SEGMENT
ORDER	PROTECTED	SELECT
OUTER	PUBLIC	SEQUENCE
OUTPUT	RAISERROR	SET
OVER	READ	SETUSER
OVERFLOW	READTEXT	SHADOW
PAD	REAL	SHARED
PAGE	REFERENCES	SHUTDOWN
PAGES	RELATIVE	SINGULAR
PARAMETER	REPLICATION	SIZE

SMALLINT	TRAILING	WAITFOR
SNAPSHOT	TRAN	WHEN
SOME	TRANSACTION	WHERE
SORT	TRANSLATE	WHILE
SPACE	TRIGGER	WITH
SQL	TRIM	WORK
SQLCODE	TRUE	WRITE
SQLERROR	TRUNCATE	WRITETEXT
STABILITY	UNCOMMITTED	YEAR
STARTING	UNION	ZONE
STARTS	UNIQUE	
STATISTICS	UPDATE	
SUBSTRING	UPDATETEXT	
SUM	UPPER	
SUSPEND	USAGE	
TABLE	USE	
TAPE	USER	
TEMP	USING	
TEMPORARY	VALUE	
TEXT	VALUES	
TEXTSIZE	VARCHAR	
THEN	VARIABLE	
TIME	VARYING	
TIMESTAMP	VIEW	
TO	VOLUME	
TOP	WAIT	

INDEX

Check out Ben's other book:

Sams Teach Yourself HomeSite 4 in 24 Hours

ISBN: 0-672-31560-2
Price: $24.99 USA / $37.95 CAN

Sams Teach Yourself HomeSite 4 in 24 Hours shows you how to create, manage, and deploy Web sites using HomeSite 4. Learn to take full advantage of the powerful HomeSite application. All the tools are covered in detail, including the edit and browse views, tree views, site management tools, color palette and graphics tools, project management, application wizards, menus, toolbars, keyboard shortcuts, and customization options. This book provides tips and tricks available in version 4.0, straight from the people who wrote the product.

- Learn to create, manage, and deploy Web sites using HomeSite 4

- CD-ROM contains a copy of HomeSite 4, evaluation versions of Macromedia DreamWeaver and ColdFusion Studio 4, and all the code from the book